THE REAL JESUS

AND

OTHER

SERMONS

By

James Allan Francis

author of, *Christ's Mould of Prayer*

and bestseller, *A Solitary Life*

Reprint edition by Dauphin Publications Inc, 2018
Cover art copyright, 2018, all rights reserved.
ISBN 978-1-939438577

Audiobook available on Audible.com

Kindle e-book available on Amazon.com

daupub.com

INTRODUCTION

WHAT would the thoughtful and reverent Christian of today not give for a sure enough close-up look at Christ Jesus as he walked among men? This is not finding fault with the Gospels but with the mass of tradition, church dogma, and what not, that has accumulated since that first century and in the mind of the church obscures the Real Jesus.

Yet we know that the only way to make him co-temporary with all the centuries is to see him in the century in which he lived. More progress has been made in the last generation in recovering the Real Saviour for human faith, than in any half dozen generations before our time.

These sermons, preached amid the pressing duties of a busy pastorate, and taken down in shorthand by a friend, represent another attempt to go back and live anew those days with Him. The old cry, "We would see Jesus" is in our hearts. If, in its limited way, this volume will help to do this for its reader the author will be grateful beyond words.

CONTENTS

Sermon I

A FULL-LENGTH PORTRAIT OF THE SON OF GOD

Consider Jesus, the Apostle and High Priest of our profession.

Hebrews 3:1

I propose for a little while this morning that we shall do exactly what this text says, "Consider Christ Jesus." You will notice that he is here given two offices or titles, that of "Apostle" and that of "high Priest." An apostle is one who comes from God to man. A high priest is one who goes from man to God. The business of an apostle is to come and speak the mind of God to man. He is a messenger. The business of a high priest is to go in and present the needs of men before God in sacrifice and intercession. In order to be a perfect apostle one must know the mind of God. In order to be a perfect high priest one must have sympathy with the needs of man. Jesus Christ is the only person who ever lived who can fill both offices perfectly, because he is the only one who combines in himself the nature of God and that of man. Having come from God, when he speaks to man he speaks with authority.

That is one of the first things people noticed when he preached. He was absolutely sure of every word. He never said, "I think" or, "May it not be so?" it was always, "Verily,

verily, I say unto you," and he did not hesitate to assume that his words had in them the finality of eternity. On the other hand, being the Son of man and able to feel all that man feels, when he approaches God on our behalf it is not only with complete knowledge but with that peculiar brand of knowledge which we call sympathy. "He knoweth our frame." You will notice that he came as God's Apostle. He went away as our High Priest. The writer of this text would have stated pretty nearly the same thing had he said, "Consider him who came, and him who went away."

The first three verses of the first chapter of Hebrews give what is probably the most complete word portrait of the Lord Jesus ever couched in one paragraph. Here we are told nine distinct things about Jesus Christ. It is easy to get hold of them for they divide themselves into three threes: Three things about his relation to the Father in heaven; three about his relation to the universe in which we live; three about his relation to our race. Here stands this man in the midst of the ages, the most remarkable phenomenon who ever crossed the horizon of this world. So great was he that no one has ever been able to take his measure. By sheer worth of character he has become the centerpiece of civilization, and today he looks in upon us from the wall whose eyes we cannot evade. More lives of Christ have been written than of anyone who ever lived, and we are only in the beginning of things yet. If we may get some clear conception of the relation of this remarkable person, first, to God; second, to creation; and third, to our human race, we shall have the basis for an intelligent faith in him.

Look now at the three statements concerning *his relation to God.* First, he is his Son. We cannot know all that this means; the mysteries of the Godhead are beyond us. Its central meaning, however, is clear. When we say that one man is another man's son, we mean that the same life derived by natural generation is in the son as is in the father. Even so, when the Scriptures say that Christ is the Son of God, whatever else it means, it certainly means that the same life that is in the Father is in the Son. I wonder if any of you are ever puzzled or troubled by the doctrine of the Trinity. I have a little formula which helps me. I hand it to you for what it is worth. It runs as follows: "All there is of God is in the Father. All that is ever seen of God is the Son. All that is ever felt of God is in the Holy Spirit." That may not be worth anything to you, but it helps me to clarify and classify things in my own mind. The Father is God. The Son is God revealed. The Spirit is God revealing. This does not clear up the mystery, of course, for here we skirt the edges of the eternal and the infinite.

Second, "He is the brightness of his glory." This illustration is borrowed from the sun. Sunlight is the brightness, the effulgence, the advertisement of the sun. Even so, Jesus Christ is the flashing forth, the very advertisement of the Father.

Third, "the express image of his person." This figure is evidently borrowed from the stamping of coins. It means something like this: You are looking at a coin. You never saw the die with which it was struck, but you know perfectly well that the coin on its face answers to the die. What the writer is saying here is that Jesus Christ is the Godhead coined in human form bearing the image and superscription of the Father. If the writer had traveled all over the field of human thought, could he have found three expressions that would more perfectly express identity of life and likeness of character than these three? "His Son," "the brightness of his glory," "the express image of his person." Christ's relation to the Father, to Eternal God, is something clearly stated for all time. The mystery of it may be beyond us, but the fact is the very bedrock of our faith in him.

Glance now at the second three, *his relation to the universe*. First, "By him God made the worlds." The truth is not so familiar as it should be. The first time we see Jesus Christ on earth he is a little child rocked in his mother's arms, like any other child, but ages before, when the universe was in its cradle, his was the hand that rocked that cradle and rocked the universe into life. He can tell the birthday of every star in the sky and every angel in heaven, for he was there and gave them birth.

Second, "He upholdeth all things by the word of his power." Science is leading us out into vast realms of natural law, we are seeing more and more clearly and orderly universe where not one atom can stray, but behind all natural laws is the Law-giver and the Law-maker. The laws of nature are the everyday habits of the Son of God. "He upholdeth all things by the word of his power."

Third, "He is the heir of all things." This carries us from the beginning of things forward to the goal toward which the whole creation moves. Everything is for him, and as the ages are wound up all their trophies will be laid at last at the feet of him who died on Calvary and who will be crowned Lord of all.

You can readily see that in these phrases the writer is not simply talking of Jesus of Nazareth, who lived for a few brief years in Galilee and Judea, he is talking of the eternal Christ who was, and is, and is to come, and who once lived on earth for a little while "for us men and our salvation."

Come now to the third three, *his relation to us*. First, He has spoken to us, "God who at sundry times and in divers manners spake in times past unto the fathers by the prophets, hath in these last days spoken unto us by his Son." The important thing in life for each one of us is to hear, understand, believe, and obey what Christ has said to us. He is the last word. It is God speaking absolute truth to our hearts through him in whom the Father is perfectly revealed.

Second, "He purged our sins." Here is the story of Calvary in four words. The transaction took place at a certain time and place in human history which we can readily name, but the atonement in the heart of God is eternal. Jesus was working out on earth and manifesting something that is the ground plan of God toward sinful humanity. Whatever else it may mean, it means that everything that is necessary to reconcile sinners to God, to purge away uncleanness and to give us victory over every sinful thing, was accomplished in that awful hour when the sufferer who hung between the thieves, bowed his head beneath the weight of the world's sin and cried, "It is finished." I am not so particular about anybody's theory of the atonement as I am about believing heartily the essential fact that God in Christ has undertaken on our behalf, and that he has not undertaken on our behalf, and that he has not undertaken in vain; that reconciliation comes not from man but from the throne; that "he has purged our sins."

And now the third item in his relation to us: "He has sat down [as our representative] at the right hand of the Majesty on High." We have a representative in heaven. We have an intercessor with God. He is the Son of Mary. He walked our earth. He ate our bread. He lived our life. He died in a human body. At the same time, he has that kind of access to God which soars so far above any human intercession in that he is the Father's beloved Son from eternity. What more do we need? God has spoken though his son a word of salvation to which nothing needs to be added. God has redeemed through

5

his Son every child of Adam by his death on Calvary and his redemption awaits the acceptance of our faith. God has placed at his own right hand One who is God glorified in human form, man glorified at the right hand of God, one "whom the Father heareth always" and "whoever liveth to make intercession for us."

This is the Christ we are to proclaim. This is the Christ we are to follow till the nations of the world come to rest beneath his shadow, and "his will is done on earth as it is in heaven."

Sermon II

AT THE COMMENCEMENT OF WORK

We have found him of whom Moses in the Law and the Prophets did write, Jesus of Nazareth
John 1:45

Istory has not been all progress. There have been periods of regression. Such a period seems to have occurred in the life of Israel in the century immediately preceding the coming of Christ. No doubt contact with Greek and afterward with Roman civilization meant some advancement in breadth of view and in creature comforts, but the old spirit that gave to Israel the eighth- and seventh-century prophets seemed to have vanished. It was a day of lesser men, a day of the rule of thumb, of minute regulations, rather than a day of great vision of God and the world. Thought, as far as it was possible, had been petrified by the pedantries and sophistries of leaders who led nowhere.

Into this lesser period with its stupid and sordid atmosphere came John the Baptist. He was regarded by the pedantic leaders of his day as a kind of religious fanatic, a man with earthquakes in his soul, who preached like thunder and lightning. Into his outdoor congregation one day, down by the Jordan, there walked the carpenter of Nazareth. He was the only man that ever awed John, that made John say, "He must increase, but I must decrease."

Two outstanding things John said concerning him. He called him "The Lamb of God," and he spoke of him as one who would "baptize with the Holy Spirit." Both of these sayings are so pregnant with meaning that it took the whole story of Jesus, indeed it has taken the centuries since to unroll the meaning wrapped up in these words. The first of these two sentences arrested the attention of two of John's followers. The name of the one was Andrew. We suspect that the other was the apostle John. Turning from John, they went directly to interview the man whom he had pointed out.

Let us make no mistake here. Jesus is standing face to face with two men. They do not know that he is the Messiah. They are not, at the moment, attaching to him any background of Old Testament prophecy. Neither do they know anything of the story of a marvelous birth. They have no preconception either against him or in his favor. The field is open. Any impression made upon them must be made by Jesus himself. He is traveling on his own merit. They said, "Master, where do you live?" With engaging frankness he replied, "Come and see," and they went home with him. It is perfectly legitimate for us, with our knowledge of him, to try as best we may to fill in, in imagination, the remainder of that day.

To sit with Jesus, to be his guest, to share his hospitality as in the home of some friend he offered it to them, to hear him talk, to ask him questions, to get his view of things, to have him lead them on a fast as they were able to go, to feel as they must have felt behind what he said the immeasurable reserve of the things he could not say yet, to bathe their souls and have their minds electrified in the atmosphere of his fresh and untrammeled thought, to listen to a man who thought as God thought, who combined the deepest respect for the traditions of their nation's past with an independence and freedom that could say, "It hath been said by them of old time, but I say unto you," to sense a man who saw the universe as the expression of his Father's love, who saw the world as the garnished and prepared home for God's children, who saw the solution of all of life's problems in the simple, all-inclusive principle of love, whose Spirit was not simply cheerful, not simply optimistic, not simply hopeful, but who saw as God saw and felt as God felt about human life here and its prospects beyond, what must it have been? He wrought no miracle that day. He was the miracle. They were dazed; they were delighted; they were made hungry for more. Little wonder that one of them found time to run away and breathlessly whisper to his brother, "We have found him, we have found him of whom Moses in the law and the prophets did write." The brother came. Another type of man altogether, a bold, impetuous, ungovernable sort of man, full of good impulses and dangerous impulses as well, the kind of man who can become great or who can become a sad shipwreck, a kind of combination of Roosevelt and Trotzky, a practical man and an idealist, a coward and a fighter, the kind of man, however, who always becomes the center in every group he enters, this man, Simon, comes into the presence of Jesus. Can you see the kind, calm, steady gaze, the combination of engaging frankness and keen insight with which he was greeted? "Your name, sir, is Simon, but henceforth your name will be the Rock." There is a combination of seriousness and playfulness. Sometimes when we want to be very complimentary we say to a man, "You are a brick," but Jesus was saying in a spirit that combined prophecy with good fellowship, "You are a rock, and that will be your name after this."

With these three next day he tramped northward across the river and entered Galilee, finding another man named Philip who belonged to the same town as Andrew and Peter. How we wish we had the whole interview. There has been preserved for us only the heart of it, two words, "Follow me." Were they words of command or only of invitation? They were both. They combine the majesty of the Saviour of the world with the free tone of one who is inviting a man to come on the inside in a great privilege. All that surrounded this remark we will have to fill in as best we may, but the sequel is the important thing. Philip obeyed. It was no accident that the disciples learned to call Jesus, Lord. He never would have received that name if he had not been Lord in deepest truth and reality. That word expressed what they felt in their deepest souls. He needed not a shred of credential for them. They saw him. They knew him, and the spell that he cast over their spirits made for them the whole world new. We cannot help but feel when people are massing proof-texts in some sort of wooden fashion to prove the deity of Christ, how utterly futile this is. No man knows Christ to be Lord unless he knows him that way, and when he knows him that way, all other proofs are unnecessary. Many years afterward one of these men wrote, "No man can say that Jesus is Lord but by the Holy Spirit."

The impression on Philip was so deep that he went to a neighbor, a friend, and said to him: "Nathanael, we have found him of whom Moses in the Law and the Prophets did write. His name is Jesus. He comes from Nazareth." Nazareth had a bad name. Nathanael, who seems to have been a thoughtful, cautious, contemplative sort of man, replies, "Can any good come out of Nazareth?" Philip said, "Come and see." Can you imagine the inflection Philip gave to those words? What Philip meant was: "It is no use for me to talk.

Come and meet him yourself, and then you will need no argument." One of the deepest metaphysical and religious principles of all life is embedded in this remark. It is just this: it is impossible for one man to share his religious experience with another. The most that any man can do for another is to put him on the clue of realizing Christ for himself, and when you have introduced the other man to Jesus, you can well be spared, indeed sometimes you are more in the way than you are of help. With each one God begins over again. Every Christian experience is a fresh edition, not a duplicate of some previous one. You can fancy the quiet, steady gaze with which Jesus looked into the eyes of Nathanael as he said, "Behold an Israelite indeed, in whom is no guile." We are not surprised at Nathanael's query, "Master, whence knowest thou me?" Then came the Master's reply, the inner meaning of which was known to Nathanael and himself and has never been fully known to anyone else: "When thou wast under the fig tree, I saw thee." Lots of guessing has been done as to what took place under that fig tree when Nathanael was there alone. It is no use to guess. Nathanael knew, and now he knew that Jesus knew. He knew that he was dealing with one who read his thoughts which had never been spoken or acted in the presence of man. Then and there he surrendered. "You are the Son of God. You are the King of Israel."

What I beg you to notice, dear friends, is that once more we have discovered that when the Lord Jesus is dealing with a human soul, his relation does not have to be propped up with any sort of outside evidence. He can make himself known in such a way that he creates a deathless faith. I gravely question if all the arguing for the deity of Christ throughout the centuries has been of any value. We do not arrive at that kind of faith by logic. It is not the child of argument. It is the child of experience. We arrive at it by

11

intuition. We often say that love constitutes its own reason. Just so faith in Jesus Christ. When communion with him has kindled your inmost soul with a light that never was on sea or land, you have a faith which needs no further proving. You would be willing to die for it. This was what happened to Nathanael. And now the Master turns and with a sweet smile says: "Because I told you that, you believe? I tell you hereafter you shall see heaven open wide, and God's angels ascending and descending upon the Son of man." This is a tremendous statement. It means: "You are accepting me as the Messiah. You are calling me Lord. The days will come when you will see that all heaven as well as earth is centered in me, and that I am not only the centerpiece of human history but the centerpiece of the plan of God." The glory of this kind of experience and this kind of knowledge of Christ is that it is not the monopoly of any privileged class either by birth, education, or temperament. It is a secret, wide open to all mankind. When the Lord Jesus calls you to all this, your experiences will not be a duplicate of Andrew's or John's or Philip's or Nathanael's. It will be yours. We have heard of a teacher who said: "in my early years, I taught subjects. There came a day when I learned to teach children." Jesus Christ is not a teacher of subjects but a tutor of souls; he is not simply a preacher of truths but a prophet of God to the inner man, God's spokesman through whom the eternal Father speaks in terms of intimate love and intimate life—giving power to the heart of his own child. Religious experience is not a machine that runs on two rails. It is an aeroplane that soars in the blue.

"This is life eternal, that they might know thee, the only true God, and Jesus Christ whom thou hast sent."

Sermon III

AS SEEN BY THE MAN WHO INTRODUCED HIM TO THE PUBLIC

Behold the Lamb of God.

He it is who baptizeth with the Holy Spirit.

John 1:29, 33

John the Baptist was the last and greatest prophet of the old dispensation and the morning star of the new, a strong, stern ascetic, a man with a backbone like a shaft of steel, coupled with a flaming heart and an eagle vision. We have no less an authority than Jesus that he was up to that time the greatest of the sons of men. What we are concerned with just now, however, is not John's personal character but his view of the Lord Jesus. Practically all that he said about him gathers around two texts.

John was preaching and baptizing in the Jordan. Crowds waited on his ministry. One day he saw in the crowd one who arrested his attention, the first and only man he ever saw to whom he could not preach repentance. He even hesitated when asked to baptize him. Shortly after, gazing upon the Master as he walked by, he said to two of his disciples (and yet he seems to be talking as much to himself as to them),

"Behold the Lamb of God which taketh away the sin of the world." John, in his thinking, was the heir of all the ages that had gone before, as this phrase "Lamb of God" bears witness. Whether blood sacrifice began as a confession of sin and an expression of desire for its removal, no one knows. It comes down from more lands than one, from prehistoric ages. Among the Jews it was elaborated into a very complicated system. The Book of Leviticus may not be very interesting to the casual reader; but to one who thoughtfully enters into the aspirations of a rude people in their upward struggle toward the light it tells a wonderful story. A blood sacrifice always meant a confession of sin upon the part of the offerer. It always meant the admission that under the government of a righteous God sin had a penalty, and it seems always to point to the double idea of substitution of the offering for the offerer and the identification of the offerer with his offering.

It is true that in the later centuries before Christ the synagogue grew up, in which the services were separated entirely from blood offerings and consisted of teaching and worship. It is true also that in the life of the people the influence of the synagogue waxed while that of the temple with its blood offerings waned. Nevertheless there still remained in the mind of Israel a connection between the blood offering and the removal of sin. John the Baptist, though rising above his age and anticipating another age, is the child of his own age, and seeing in Jesus something in relation to God and man that the rest of men were very slow to see, he cried, "Behold the Lamb of God that beareth away the sin of the world."

You can always tell something about the size of a person by the task that is set for him or that he sets for himself. I will ask you now to measure Jesus Christ by the task that John set for him. It was a task that had baffled the ages. To come in between God and man, to make such an adjustment in his own person between God and sinful humanity as to remove the embarrassment which sin causes in the heart of every one who tries to approach God, so that he who knows he has sinned can come into the presence of God not only without dread, but with the sense of a great welcome; to reconcile God to man in every sense in which he needs reconciliation, this is a task not for a man or a superman, but for one who combines in himself essential manhood and essential Godhood. The difficulty with any theory of the atonement is the difficulty of making it ample enough to include all the facts and make all the provisions necessarily involved in the awful mystery of sin. If the Lord Jesus can really do what John said, it goes a long way toward determining who and what he is. Are we prepared to believe that all the millions who have found peace through him have been deceived, that the hymnology of the ages concerning the Cross is but an empty dream? Mark well, my hearer, if it is true that the Son of God is also the Lamb of God, that he has vital relations with your soul in the matter of reconciliation with God and in the removal of sin and its stains, then this is not a matter to be passed by lightly, like a game of golf, as optional. Rather it is a matter of eternal life or death.

Turn now to the second great text, "The same is he that baptizeth with the Holy Spirit." One of the most familiar conceptions of Jesus is as an example for humanity, the perfect life once lived that men may follow his steps. Did it ever occur to you that if Jesus was this and nothing more, he would be the everlasting despair of mankind? What good is a perfect example to me if I am expected perfectly to follow it? I started *toward* God, but here is a man who started *from* God. The attainments which I by grace painfully achieve seemed to be his naturally. But when I turn to this great text,

I discover that Jesus is something more than an example. Besides showing me an illustrious and splendid example to follow, he offers me a life to be shared. He comes and clothes my poor sinful spirit, with its weakness and waywardness, with his own Spirit. We are all familiar with the idea that when two people learn to love each other, spirit flows over and interpenetrates spirit. The highest example of this in the universe is the dealing of Christ with the souls of men. He interpenetrates our life until we can not only say, "I am in Christ," but "Christ liveth in me." The most perfect illustration you can find in human life of the very thought and feeling of one person being imparted to another falls far short of what Christ can do in the humblest heart.

Once again, we say, you can judge something of who and what he is by the task that is set for him. Who is this that can clothe the millions of our race with a Spirit divine? Who is this that can be the distributor of that royal bounty of God, not the distributor of such material things as bread and meat, but the distributor of that Spirit which is at the heart of the universe, this infinite Spirit of love that moved God to create the worlds, to create mankind, to bear patiently with their waywardness and wickedness, to brood over them in holy love through the centuries, to reveal himself to them and in Christ to place himself at their disposal even unto death? Who is this, I say, who is the distributor of this Spirit, saying to each of us, "I am come that ye might have life, and that ye might have it more abundantly"? I would stake the absolute divinity of Jesus Christ on these two texts alone. The one who can remove the sin of the world by reconciling a sinning soul to God, and who can clothe that soul permanently with the beauty of heaven by imparting to it the very life of God, is something more than the Son of Mary. He is something more than the most illustrious in the census of this world.

This fact that God could be incarnated in a real man, dignifies the entire human race. Who could think meanly of human nature when it is the very nature in which he dwelt and which he has glorified in his own person far above all things.

Has the Lord Jesus done these two things for you? Has he so reconciled you to God that the perfect, fatherly love of God has become real to you? Does he so assist you by his Spirit that the "I must" of law becomes the "I can" of grace? If not, he waits for the acceptance of your faith, for the surrender of your will that he may work in you to will and to do of his good pleasure. Give yourself a chance. Believe the glorious gospel, believe it now, believe it for your own life and your own difficulties. Believe it in such a way as to say, "Thank God I do not have to be the kind of a man or woman that I have been."

And that which seemed to me before
One wild, confused Babel,
Is now a fire-tongued Pentecost
Proclaiming Christ is able,
And all creation its evangel
Utters forth abroad
Into mine ears
Since once I know
My Saviour Christ is God.

Sermon IV

AS SEEN BY HIS BEST FRIEND

In the beginning was the Word.

No man hath seen God at any time; the only begotten Son, which is in the bosom of the Father, He hath declared him.
John 1:1, 18

There is a reason to think of John as the youngest of the Twelve, a youth among bearded men. Whether for this reason or because of a naturally greater capacity for affection, he seems nearer to the Master than the rest. He was known as "the disciple whom Jesus loved." He had three unforgettable years of the most intimate acquaintance possible with him and then perhaps a half century of deepest fellowship in the Spirit after Jesus had left the world. He outlived all the apostles and probably wrote his Gospel after they were all gone and after the other three Gospels had become fairly well known throughout the churches. It would be quite worthwhile to see how the Lord Jesus looked to his closest friend after these long years of service and meditation.

They first met yonder by the river where John the Baptist was preaching. He had said some wonderful things about the Master, declaring that he himself was unworthy even to unloose the latchet of his shoes. On that first day of acquaintance Jesus invited the young man to go home with him. To him then, Jesus was just a man and a prophet, but he soon began to see and hear things which overflowed all the measures of manhood, of even perfect manhood. The wonder of his words and deeds, his evident sense of at-homeness in the heavenly world, the transfiguration scene, puzzled John and filled him with an awe that was worship. The longer he followed him the more clear it became to him that while Jesus was a real man, he was something more.

Then came his awful death and triumphant resurrection. John, like the others, became certain that his Master had survived death, not as any man may hope to survive, simply by continued existence somewhere beyond the grave, but as one who had conquered death and now lived as a universal and eternal presence. Very naturally would come the thought, If Calvary was not the end, and it certainly was not, then Bethlehem was not the beginning.

Besides this John vividly remembered saying of the Master which pointed back to a life he had lived before he was born of Mary: "I came down from heaven;" "I came forth from the Father;" "What and if ye shall see the Son of man ascend up where he was before?" "Father, glorify thou me with thine own self with the glory which I had with thee before the world was." All this led John and the others to see that Jesus' earthly life was an episode between two eternities, one stretching back before all worlds and the other forward forever. In short, they came to see that they were not swelling with a created being higher and better than themselves but with one who was from everlasting to everlasting.

Now arose the big question. What then is the relation between God the Father and this eternal Christ whom John knew by the human name of Jesus? Here John picks up a word used by none of the other three Gospel writers. The word probably came from Alexandria. Alexandria was then the second city in the world. One-fifth of its population were

Jews. It was a great philosophic and literary center. The Jews resident in Alexandria had, during the centuries of their stay in Egypt, absorbed much Greek philosophy. They had translated the Old Testament into Greek, the version, by the way, from which the Lord Jesus usually quoted. Their scholars had set themselves to the task of interpreting Hebrew theology, that is, the Old Testament, in terms of Greek philosophy.

It would be a wearisome tale to follow the story. They thought they had succeeded. About twenty years before the birth of Christ, there was born among them in Alexandria a very remarkable man. His name was Philo. He wrote much, and his fame was wide. We do not know as much of him as we should like. He lived till A.D. 54. Once when the Egyptian Jews sent a delegation to Caligula the emperor to ask that they be not compelled to worship the emperor's statue, Philo was their unsuccessful spokesman.

His idea was that God—the ultimate God—had nothing directly to do with the universe, either in creation or management, but that he acted through an emanation, sometimes regarded as personal and sometimes as impersonal, whom he called the "Logos," or as we say in English, "the Word." Amid the mass of fancies Philo and his school wove around this expression, there was one great idea. We may phrase it somewhat as follows: A word is more than the expression of an idea, it is the expression of the person who holds the idea. Our words reveal us. When a man opens his mouth, character rushes out of doors and advertises itself. If you could take all the words a man speaks from the beginning of his life to the end of it and condense them into one great, big word that would include in its meaning all that he had ever said, that word would represent him. This "Logos" of Philo was such a word from God.

This word and its meaning had traveled far around that East-Mediterranean world in the years that intervened. John did not live in a mental vacuum. Woe to the man who tries to be a teacher without being a student and thinker.

John takes up this expression, "The Logos," and sloughing off the puerile fancies with which Philo and his school had clothed it, and putting into it a fullness of meaning by the inspiration of the Holy Spirit of which Philo never dreamed, John calls Jesus "The Logos." It is as if he said: "If the whole character of eternal God, his heart, his mind, his purpose in the universe, were condensed into one great word that would rightly represent him, that word would be Jesus Christ. He is the living word of God." We will get at John's meaning best by rereading the eighteenth verse of this chapter: "No man hath seen God at any time. The only begotten Son, which is in the bosom of the Father, he hath *declared him*."

Then Jesus Christ is God expressed, God translated into human terms. John even goes back to the beginning and declares that the eternal Word, Christ, is the active expression of God in Creation as well as in providence, revelation, and redemption. "All things were made by him, and without him was not anything made that was made."

We come now to the question of questions for us sons of men. John, you saw and heard him. You know him better than any other man. You often leaned your head upon his breast. You say he is the very revelation of God. Tell us, pray, what kind of character did you see in him? After three years of walking with him, and a whole generation of time to ponder his words and deeds, if he is to you the very unveiling of the Father, what is he like?

Twice in these two great verses, John answers us in the same words, "Full of grace and reality." (I use the word "reality" instead of "truth" not to change the meaning but to compel attention to the real meaning.) Let us look closely at these two great words in which John, the beloved, describes his Master.

Reality. Then Jesus is no painted ship on a painted ocean, no actor playing a part. He is the reality of God. When John leaned his cheek on Jesus' heart yonder at supper, he was against the beating heart of God. No need to go farther. There is not farther to go. When you have found Jesus you have found God.

Now look at the other word: *Grace*. Someone says, "Oh, that means love." Wait! Wait! A young man meets a face in the crowd. The whole of life is changed for him. He gives her his heart and hand. That is a beautiful thing, but it is not grace. Wherein is the difference? It is here. He loves her for something he sees or thinks he sees in her. But Jesus Christ loves people who are absolutely unlovely, unsightly, disgusting people that it is painful for him to have anything to do with, yet he loves them; but his love is founded not on any attractiveness in them but on what he is in himself. His love rests not on what he sees in us but has its foundation in his own nature, his own infinite heart of love. He loved Judas when he was hanging on the cross to which Judas had betrayed him. If that man, instead of hanging himself, had come back after Jesus rose from the dead and had thrown himself at Jesus' feet for mercy, he would be among the saints in heaven today. Grace is that kind of love in Jesus that assures me that I do not have to be worthy to be loved, in order to be forgiven, in order to be saved, in order to enter his fellowship.

Jesus must be true to himself, and his nature is such that he looks upon his murderers and cries, "Father, forgive them, for they know not what they do." I had rather undertake to measure anything in time or eternity than to try to measure the grace of Christ. After John has gazed on him the flesh during the years of his ministry and then through the Spirit for well-nigh half a century, he can find no words to describe him save these, "Full of grace and reality."

John, just one more question. If I receive him, believe on him, attach myself to him, surrender my life into his keeping, what will he "put across" to me? Listen carefully here to John's answer: "And of his fullness have all we received and grace upon grace." Christ not only can love, but he has the ability to create in us the same kind of gracious disposition we have seen in him so that we may love with his kind of love. John puts it another way, "To as many as received him, to them gave he the power to become the sons of God, even to them that believe on his name, which were born, not of blood, nor of the will of the flesh, nor of the will of men, but of God." Here we reach God's goal: That the love-life of Christ should be so imparted to men as to awaken in them a love for others like his, making them the sons of God in deed and in truth. It was for this Christ came to earth. This is the gospel with which we are entrusted today for the whole world.

Sermon V

DEALING WITH TEMPTATION

*Tempted in all points like as we are, yet
without sin.*

Hebrews 4:15

It was 27 A.D. A man was working in a carpenter shop in the village of Nazareth on the plain of Esdraelon. Palestine was seething with discontent. Rumors of risings and rebellions followed one another, each in turn to be quenched in blood by the iron hand of Rome. They young carpenter allows them all to pass and allies himself with none. Presently a new rumor comes. A prophet has arisen. He is not a politician at all. He is preaching, not against Rome, but against sin, and his ringing slogan is, "Repent, for the reign of God is near!" those who respond to his message are baptized as a striking confession that they renounce their old life and are born into a new sphere. Now the carpenter leaves the shop, travels to the Jordan, and offers himself for baptism. His baptism does not mean the renouncing of personal sin. He is the one sinless man in history, and he knows it. It is, however, a confession of his people's sins and his complete identification of himself with them. It is also his solemn and deliberate consecration of himself to what he regards as his life-work. John's hesitation is overruled by one quiet word, and then the Lord from heaven is baptized by a man. This was accompanied by a spiritual experience. He heard a voice from heaven, "This is my beloved Son in whom I am well pleased," and there came upon him an enduement of spiritual power without measure. With this seems to have come the fulness of a threefold consciousness. We say the "fulness," for we believe that this consciousness had been growing upon him through the years. It seems now to have ripened into fullness. First, the sense of a unique relationship to God, that of being God's only begotten Son: secondly, the sense that upon him was laid the task of being the World's Saviour, the Messiah; thirdly, the consciousness that his personal life was to set the pace for all men and for all the centuries; that

> The ebbs and flows of his single soul
> Were tides to the rest of mankind.

Is it any wonder that in that awful hour he turned away from everybody he had ever known and went out into the wilderness to think? Let us for a few minutes reverently watch what transpires there. We probably have the story in his own words. There was no way that the disciples could ever know about it except as he told them. Here we are confronted with the kind of embarrassment that fills us with awe. We can more or less measure what goes on in the souls of men who are our equals. We judge them by ourselves and rightly so, but where is the plumb-line with which to measure the depth of his experience? We are looking this morning at a sinless man who knows himself to the Son of God, who knows that he is the Saviour the world has waited for since the world was young, and who knows that his actions will be set up as a standard to be appealed to in all lands until time shall be no more. There is one type of mind that amazes me, and that is the mind that can be cocksure about everything in the presence of such realities as these. I can only say to such,

I tread with bare, hushed feet the ground
Ye tread with boldness shod.

The fact that he was tempted makes him my neighbor
and draws me close to him, makes me feel that I can learn
something from him, makes him a real man on the human
side. But the other side of his life reaches away out into the
eternal, beyond my ken. Instead of saying, "That's that," after
the fashion of men who can account for everything from
natural phenomena, I rather tread as with unshod feet the
courts of an invisible temple and let wonder have its full
share in my thinking.

A man can only be tempted on the plane on which he
lives. The coarse temptations that make a strong appeal to
vulgar natures make no appeal at all to the refined. This is
true of Jesus. So completely is he now identified with and
consecrated to the work of the kingdom that if he can be
tempted at all, it will be concerning the nature of that
kingdom. A series of alternatives present themselves to him.
He is compelled to choose and so far as we can see, through
all his afterlife, he never wavered for one second from the
great decisions taken there in the Judean wilderness.

The three temptations recorded have one thing common
to all three, and that is the temptation to take himself out of
the Father's hands and take short cut of his own choosing
toward the desired goal.

Let us look carefully at these three in turn. He is hungry.
The desert beneath his feet is covered with little stones
shaped very much like the little loaves to which he had been
used. Why not, with his consciousness of power, turn some
of them into loaves and supply his hunger? There are here
several temptations in one. It means taking himself out of the

Father's hands instead of living the life of personal trust, it means refusing to accept the common lot of men who have to trust an unseen Father, and it means putting the physical before the spiritual. I wonder how far ahead he looked. Did he see that this last would be the temptation that would overcome the majority of men through all time? We have only to look around us today to see how large physical comfort bulks in the mind of the average man or woman as compared with spiritual experience. There came to his mind an ancient scripture, "Man doth not live by bread alone, but by every word that proceedeth out of the mouth of God." It is not a question of whether man is partly spiritual and partly physical. The Master knew that. It is a question of which comes first, and Jesus then and there rightly reading the soul of man, fills the unrolled page of future history when he decides that in his kingdom the spiritual shall come first. Let me ask you, do you feel that because you have enough and to spare of material goods, because you have a home with its comforts, an auto to use for pleasure or profit, you do not need the worship of God, the fellowship of his people, and the stimulus of his word? We are in great danger in the United States of America just because of our prosperity. It verily seems that the more the Lord does for people, the less they love him. We are apt to allow the good gifts of his hands to stand between us and fellowship with his heart. It is more important for us to know God through his word than it is to have this or that material good.

The second great alternative presents itself in a most dramatic way. It is the suggestion that because he is in the divine care, because he knows the promises of God for his protection are sure, he should presume thereon and use his power as magic to produce supernatural, stunning wonders to enhance his own popularity. Jump from the pinnacle of the temple—and there even came to mind a verse in one of the psalms, "He shall give his angels charge over thee to keep thee, and in their hands they shall bear thee up lest thou dash thy food against a stone." Clearly two alternatives present themselves to him. Shall he use spiritual power simply as a magical wonder-worker, or shall it be all under the control of right reason and moral purpose? The Master's decision is taken at once. He couches it in the language of another ancient scripture, "Thou shalt not presumptuously try the Lord thy God."

The third temptation here mentioned was undoubtedly the climax. It is concerning his method of world conquest. The suggestion is that he fall down and worship Satan. We must read between these lines. We must read under them; we must read behind them. Jesus did not live in a vacuum. His mind was alertly in touch with the world of his day. The largest success on the world's map at that time, and the largest success that had ever been on the map, was the Roman Empire. Caesar, in his gilded palace on the Tiber, ruled with an iron hand the civilized part of mankind and even the fringes of barbarism. The suggestion is: "Master, you expect your kingdom to be universal. That is your desire. Take a leaf out of Rome's book. All power is yours. No kingdom has ever been built up in this world this far except by the sword. Compromise with that power. Make yours another larger, better, juster Roman Empire, but built substantially by the same methods." Can you see how subtle and almost overpowering this temptation was? It is so much easier to follow a precedent than to break new ground. Master, think you to build your kingdom in the hearts of men wholly by the persuasion of love? It will be a slow process. "Even so," thinks Jesus, "I have plenty of time. The ages belong to me"—and then and there he made the decision which has ruled in his kingdom so far as he had been obeyed from that day to his, that no attempt would ever be made to coerce men into believing or obeying him. The kingdom of God has no press-gang. You come in as a volunteer or not at all, and after you are in you stay in as a volunteer. Once when many left him, he turned to the disciples and said, "Will ye also go away?" There was nothing to hinder them except their attachment to him. Our Lord Jesus has no faith in any method of holding people except by the charm if his own personality and the gentle might of his grace. What do you think, after nineteen centuries, of the wisdom of his decision? Let's look around us a little and see. Where's the Roman Empire now? You must dig in the dusty pages of forgotten history to find its story. And where is the kingdom of Christ now? It confronts you at every crossroads, in every crowded mart, and in every realm of human thought and activity across the face of the world, and it is only in its infancy compared with what it will be in the days that are ahead. Lord Jesus, we bow at thy feet in silent wonder, awe, and worship. Thou art the seer of seers, at the beginning thou didst arrive at the decisions which will be universal at the end. Thou alone hast no need to change thy mind or reverse thy purposes.

Dear friend, what does it mean to you that Jesus Christ, was tempted in all points like as you are? He is asking you to follow him today. Please remember, however, for your comfort and help that in following Jesus, you are not following an ancient model, but a living, present friend. No one can follow Jesus with an even partial success who simply sees him as a historic figure. It is the personal fellowship of a living friend that makes possible discipleship.

The Saviour comes and walks with me,
And sweet communion here have we.

If this is your experience and mine, then the might of the Creator of the world becomes to us the might of the Saviour of the world, and a power is exerted in us and on our behalf though grace that is equal to the power witnessed in creation and providence. When the telescope reveals a system of worlds so far away that it takes light, traveling 186,000 miles a second, ten millions of years to come from those stars to us, let us just remember that all this is his garden, his creation, that he holds them in the hollow of his hand, and that the same voice which created and controls them says to you and to me, "Come unto me and I will give you rest," and the hand of the Architect of the skies has become the pierced hand of the Saviour of men.

Sermon VI

DEALING WITH HELPLESS MORAL DERELICT

If thou knewst the gift of God.

John 4:10

When we watch the Master dealing with the Twelve, he is dealing not with perfect men but with normal, average relationships with society. This morning I am going to ask you to turn aside from that and behold Jesus dealing with one who had lost out in the race of life, who had become so entangled in sin and shame, that neither she nor the community in which she lived could see any way back for her. My reasons for asking you to look at this particular case are these: first, because there is more kinship between ourselves and a woman like this than we at first like to admit; and second, we never see the real romance of divine grace until God at his best meets human nature at its worst.

The Master had been preaching in Judea and was passing through the intervening territory of Samaria toward Galilee. He stopped at noon by a wellside to rest, and sent his disciples to a near-by village to get some food. While they were gone, out from the village yonder came a woman with a water-jar to draw water. We might just as well tell the cold truth about her at once. Society has its standards, and woe to the person who defies them. This woman had so far outraged the standards of her time and country she had become a human pariah. We do not know whether she was more sinned against than sinning, or how she came to fall. It may be that if we knew the whole story, we would say that a combination of circumstances had pushed her down until she had joined that class of women who in a fearful sense bear the sins of the world and the curse that goes with them.

She had been married five times and was now living with a man who was not her husband at all. She had been cast out of decent society, and the door was shut and barred. The grave, and a dishonored grave at that, was her only hope.

She approached the well where Jesus was sitting. He was tired. He was hungry. He was thirsty. All that she saw was a Jew. Race hatred is a very common thing in the world even today, but we have to look long and far for a race hatred more bitter than that between the Jew and the Samaritan. They were a kind of cousins, the Jew representing what was left of the old Southern kingdom, and the Samaritan the old Northern kingdom. To a race hatred was added a religious hatred. She so shares this that the moment she sees him, though she personally has no religion, her heart is filled with an antipathy that cannot be put into words.

Mark now Jesus' behaviour. He opened the conversation, quite an unusual thing, for men did not speak to women in public, especially to such as she. He opened it in the most adroit and diplomatic way imaginable. He asked her for a favor, just a drink of water. The likelihood is that he had not spoken until after she had drawn the water from the well, but as she rests the dripping jar on the well-curb, ready in another minute to put it on her shoulder and be away, he said, "Give me to drink."

That should have helped to soften her, but her answer showed mingled indignation and surprise. "How is it that thou, being a Jew, askest this drink of me, which am a woman of Samaria?" for the Jews have no dealings with the Samaritans.

The door of opportunity is wide open now, and the Master replies. His answer for beauty and tenderness defies description. It is the art of heaven. It is the gentleness of God. He assumes her need. He assumes God's fullness of supply of grace, he assumes God's willingness, and he assumes that he is the medium through whom God can reach her.

"If thou knewest the gift of God and who it is who talketh with thee, thou wouldst have asked of him, and he would have given thee living water." These words and the manner in which he spoke them defy description—skill, sympathy, gentleness, kindness, authority. Who can paint the lily? Who can gild the sunbeam? If we dared to say it, we would say, "That is Jesus at his best."

The woman knows that she is needy, but she does not feel it as much as she will in a few minutes. She knows that God is gracious, but if the question were raised, "Could the grace of God reach her?" she would hesitate. She had become so entangled in the meshes of sin that good people felt they could not afford to have anything to do with her. Very naturally she would feel that God felt the same way. The social engineer of our day would have begun by inquiring into the social system that produced such a life as unfortunate as hers, and then would have said, "It is time for us to make some new law." I have no fault to find with this. It may reach very far and do uncounted thousands good in the years to come. But Jesus is Master of the direct method. He stops not to inquire how she came to be in this condition; how far she is to blame, or how far astray. He has a road that is as direct as the will of God. He knows that God in his infinite grace has something to give her, and if she receives that it will change her whole life.

Horace Bushnell once said, "The soul of all improvement is the improvement of the soul." He got that from Jesus. Jesus never said these words, but he acted them. Looking into the face of this woman who had crossed that line which, when a woman crosses she very seldom comes back in this world, he never thought of being discouraged, but quietly said, "If thou knewest the gift of God and who it is that talketh with thee, thou wouldest have asked of him, and he would have given thee living water."

When her answer came it showed that she was still in the dark, but her heart was beginning to melt. She did not understand what he said, but she felt the way he said it. She thinks he is talking of some extraordinary water better than the water in the well, but his kindness is changing the climate of the world for her.

"Sir, thou hast nothing to draw with and this is a deep well. From whence then hast thou that living water? Art thou greater than our father, Jacob, who gave us the well and drank therefrom himself, and his children, and his cattle?"

His second answer completes the first: "Whosoever drinketh of this water shall thirst again, but whosoever drinketh of the water that I shall give him, shall never thirst. It shall become in him a well of water springing up unto everlasting life."

What is this Jesus is saying? His cure for the satisfaction of sin is a greater satisfaction. Sin keeps its grip on us by the satisfactions which it brings. That is where its enticement lies. His cure for sin is to give something that gives far greater satisfaction.

You might have gathered all the folks in Samaria good and bad, and put this woman's case before them and said: "Here is a woman who has been turned out by one husband after another five times, and now she is living with another man who is willing to pay her board. What shall we do with her? "They will reply: "It is very difficult question. If it were not for the prejudices that people have, a certain peculiar antipathy to those who have fallen in that way, something might be done. She has gone so far that it has ceased to seem wrong to her. If it wasn't that this woman's sense of shame," etc., etc., and you can keep on all day, "If it wasn't" this or that, and end with "We can see no way of restoring her."

Jesus comes. There were no books on psychology then, but he knew the human heart. The heart of every fine thing that we've learned in psychology was anticipated by him. He takes up her case. He does not change a law. He does not alter a custom. He changes her, and he does it by bringing her to God and bringing God to her, and when he brought her face to face with the eternal God and told her that God through him would give her living water, the connection by faith was made. Her whole outlook on life was changed, and she cried out, "Master, give me this water."

She hardly knows what she is asking, but she is a suppliant just the same. Then the Master put his finger tenderly but very frankly on the sorest spot in her life. "Go call thy husband and come hither." I beg you to notice that the disciples were not there. They were alone. "I have no husband." "Thou hast well said I have no husband, for thou hast had five husbands, and he whom thou now hast is not thy husband." It is hard to hear such a statement, even though made with the kindness of Jesus. She tried to evade the issue. Don't blame her. Most of us would have done the same had we been in her place. She turns to the old dispute between Jew and Samaritan about the proper place for worship, "Our fathers worshipped in this mountain, and ye say that in Jerusalem is the place where men ought to worship."

The Master says nothing more about the man who is not her husband, but turns to the new topic of conversation which she has introduced, and in five minutes he tells her more about the nature of worship than all the sages had said up to that time. He revealed to her the ultimate truth of the matter: "God is spirit; and they that worship him must worship in spirit and in truth." As if he would say: "Woman, you do not have to go to Jerusalem or Gerizim or anywhere else. The only thing that matters in worship is the attitude of your heart toward God."

Indeed the air to which he had lifted her was too rare for her as yet and she fairly gasped out: "Well, I know the Messiah cometh which is called Christ. When he is come he will tell us all things." And then Jesus told her the mighty secret that he very seldom told anybody; he said, "I that speak unto you am he."

She never waited for another word. She left her water-jar standing where it was, and on swift feet she was away to town. She approached the men. The women would not have listened to her. I think I can see the leer on the face of some low fellow as they see her coming, the rude joke is all ready to spring to his lips, but she had not been talking to those men five minutes before the lowest man in that crowd knew in his wretched soul that the last rude familiarity with that woman was over forever. She says: "Come, see a man who has told me all that I ever did. Is not he the Messiah?" and in almost less time than it takes to tell it she had the village on the move.

Behold how far this woman has traveled from what she was at the beginning of the story! Then she was a piece of human wreckage who had lost hope herself, and everybody had lost hope for her. Now she is the messenger of Jesus. She needs no credentials. The new spirit that had clothed her life and that was evident to all, was credential enough. This is the grace of God at work. This is Jesus Christ doing what he came into this world to do, to change human lives from sin to holiness, from despair to hope, from weakness to strength, from being accursed and a curse to being a stream of blessing.

They came. They listened. They said to the woman, "Now we believe, not because of thy saying, for we have heard him ourselves, and we know indeed that this is the Christ, the Saviour of the world."

Probably no group there was more astonished than the disciples. They had yet to learn how long is mercy's reach and how strong is mercy's arm. They had yet to learn that the clemency of God is greater than the malignity of the devil, and that Jesus can match and overmatch the effect of years of sinful habit and can create right out of the dust and mire of a sinful life the morning of eternal life, the beginnings of heaven on earth the kingdom of God in man.

Sermon VII

THE FORGIVENESS OF SIN

He said unto her, thy sins are forgiven.

Luke 7:48

From the Apostles' Creed you read, "I believe in the forgiveness of sins." I should like to talk to you this morning about this very important matter. Sir Oliver Lodge has said, "The modern man is so busy that he has no time to think of his sins." Another has replied, "If sin is as serious a thing as it has been taken to be through all ages, then it is a pity that the modern man is so short of time." I think you will all agree with me that throughout the entire history of the world sin has been the most serious problem that has ever confronted mankind, and it is not a whit less serious now than ever before.

We change the terms, we alter the phraseology, but that does not change the thing itself. We call it by different names, but that does not eliminate the thing. It is astonishing how men try to "pooh, pooh" the thing out of court. Walt Whitman said he enjoyed the company of cows more than he did that of men because cows just chew their cud and don't talk about their sins. That may have been a very profound remark, but to me it is very foolish and superficial. No, cows do not talk about their sins. Man is the only being that can interfere with the moral order of the universe. Hence, he is the only being on earth that has this problem confronting him. After we have said all the smart things we can say and tried to evade the issue in Christian Science fashion, by ignoring the real facts, after we have gone through all that, if we open our eyes, look around, and see the number of broken lives and the amount of tragedy that is engrained in this world because of sin, we should realize that evasion or denial is not a remedy.

It is my lot frequently to speak to high-school audiences, hundreds of boys and girls, overflowing with life, full of high hope, every one expecting to succeed and make a shining mark in the world. Behind them I see a great company of fathers and mothers, fondly hoping and saying: "I am sure he is going to succeed. I know I can count on him. I know I shall be proud of him."

If you and I could see this same great company forty years from now, how many of them would we find had fulfilled the splendid promise of their youth, and how many turned out to be disappointments to themselves, their parents, and their friends?

What is behind all this? There is one answer. Sin. Don't try to minimize it. That doesn't cure it at all. The reason that more earnest, concentrated thinking has been done concerning the death of Jesus than concerning any other fact in human history is because man has believed that the death of Christ has something to do with the remedy for human sin.

Why pick out the Galilean carpenter, who died on the cross between two thieves? Why should a multitude of intelligent and reverent people turn their eyes to that cross ever since? The answer is that we believe that away back there his death had something very important to do with the world's greatest and most tragic problem.

Before I go any farther, I am going to ask you once more, as you value your own Christian sanity, not to yield to the tendency of our day to make light of sin. It is not common sense. It is not righteousness. It is not truth. It is nothing but sheer idiocy.

There are many ways of looking at sin. I will mention only three: First, you may regard it as a bad record that you have on high and that you would like to have blotted out. That is the most superficial view of sin. If you do not see anything as forgiveness but a trick of bookkeeping at the right hand of God, so that somehow the record of sin is blotted out, expunged, deleted, as we said during the war, you have not sounded the depths of its meaning at all. Granted this view of sin is true as far as its goes, a man with a bad record would be glad to have it blotted out, and he hopes somehow that God will blot it out and leave him with a clean sheet so that someday he can stand before him unashamed; but this is far from being the whole story.

Secondly, besides the record on high, sin leaves a record in your own bosom. It is a record that is woven into the very tissues of your being and every fiber and nerve of your body, and into the inner chambers of your soul. The name of this awful record is *habit*. Suppose the record in heaven is wiped out, and there is no change in heart, am I delivered from sin? Supposed God does in his mercy expunge or delete the record that was made in heaven, and I enter into heaven just the same man I was when I committed the sin, carrying with me the whole outfit of evil habits that I have formed, I would not be any better off in heaven than I would be in Los Angeles. If eternal God is really going to tackle the problem of human sin for us men and do a really efficient job, he must deal with this whole outfit of habits that I have formed.

There is a third view—the influence that my sin has made on the lives of others—the influence which has gone from me, and which I have no power now to change, no matter how truly I repent.

Let me take an awful illustration, a case that I happen to know well. A young man contracted a disease that we do not talk about in good society, and then—crime upon crime—he married a good, pure girl. She became diseased. He took treatment, was cured, and is a healthy man today. She and her little child both rotted in a loathsome death. Yes, he got it out of his system, but how about her? How about the little child that was damned into life rather than born?

If you could turn away from every wrong thing that you have ever done and live from now on an absolutely straight life, how about the influence you have exerted against others, which is going on and on and on? Have you quite cleaned up the whole thing while that is going on in another man's life out there? Don't you see what a far-reaching thing sin is? I wish that today we could all get away from the superficial way of looking at sin. Some people seem to think that divine forgiveness is something like this: As I am boarding a car a man steps on my foot. As I look up, he begs my pardon, and I say, "All right." But, suppose that the same man ruins my little girl and comes round and begs my pardon, do I say, "All right"?

I don't believe that there has been a generation of people in the world for a thousand years so much in danger of the superficial view of sin as the generation to which we belong. Sin is a joke on the stage. Largely so in the public press, whether newspaper or book literature. When I see long lines of people standing waiting for tickets before a moving-picture house, I ask myself what kind of things are impressed on their minds in there. Is it generally that sin is a huge, funny joke?

We find the same thing in the press. The war is "the late unpleasantness," and everything else is treated in like manner. We ought not to get our ideas of sin, its peril, and cure from the society around us, but from Him.

There is a certain man whom we call "the man on the street," by which we mean the rough-and-tumble sort of man who eats three square meals a day. He is here because he's here, and he does not know why. If you ask him where he is going, he says, "I am on my way, but I don't know where." There is none quicker to give his opinion of sin than that man, and it is worth just about the time it took him to arrive at it, less than sixty seconds.

There are great souls who have thought deeply and lived earnestly and tried to do the will of God. These have the strongest sense of sin. It is the person who has not thought deeply or lived earnestly or tried to do the will of God who is almost minus the sense of sin.

Turn the light in on your own soul and ask: "What has sin done for me?" "What has the sin of others done for me?" "What has my sin done for others?" "What has my sin done to God and his great purpose in life?"

Turn back now to those three views of sin! The first, that you have a bad record on high that you would like to have blotted out; the second, that sin has also left a record written on the inner chambers of your soul in the very fiber of your being; the third, that sin is an influence which you have started and by which you have affected for ill the lives of others.

Take the first, "the bad record on high." I am not using the word with slavish literalness. None of us think of literal books on the desk beside God's throne. Nevertheless, the metaphor is correct and it gives a correct idea, namely, that we have a bad record in heaven, and we are very desirous of having that record expunged. Suppose then that I can be assured that the books of heaven are all fixed, and that nothing stands against me, that the angels stand at the gate to welcome me. I have but touched the fringe of the matter of my own personal sin because the difficult problem is not up there, but in here.

Sin is gratifying and pleasing of self in defiance of God's moral law, the laws of nature, and the laws of my own being. There is one Law-giver, and one supreme law, and when I go against that I go against not only God but nature and my own best self for selfish gratification. You and I were built for God and built for others. The human will is made for fellowship with him and fellowship with each other in his fellowship. When I turn from fellowship with God and try to live without him, and turn from the service of others, saying, "I am going to gratify myself, I am going to look out for number one," I am enthroning self in the place God ought to occupy. I am a sinner.

Take the case of the Pharisees and the woman whom they brought into the Master's presence with accusation. I have no manner of doubt that when the record says she was a sinner, it tells the truth. She had sinned in ways we had better not discuss. But what about those Pharisees? They had not been indulging in her kind of sin, but when it came to putting self ahead of God and ahead of others they had far eclipsed her record of guilt.

I need not only a divine mercy which will blot out the bad record against me, but I need something more. I need mercy in the form of divine efficiency that will take hold and help me to get things right in my own bosom, that will enable me to change my inner habits of thought and purpose so that I shall deliberately choose the will of God and live in it rather than seek my own gratification in defiance of his will. I had better not try to separate these two. God never blots out a bad record without doing something more. Never!

I can see in memory now the figure of a man I used to know in my boyhood. He kept an illicit saloon in a town and country that was dry. That is, he was doing an absolutely illegitimate business. He kept his saloon open all week and until 12 o'clock on Saturday night to make gain for himself at the expense of the ruin of the young men of that town; but at 6 o'clock Sunday morning, neatly groomed, shaved and dressed, I would see him make his way up to the church to confession to have a smile so broad that he almost had to move his ears back to make room for it. However, promptly at 2 o'clock on Sunday afternoon the side door opened and the process of the week before was repeated. Do you believe that eternal God indulges in any such stupid jugglery as that? A repentance that is not coupled with a change in the inner determination of the soul, in the purposes and the habits of thought, is not repentance at all.

Now let us say as clearly as we may, what shall I do concerning the record up yonder? I can't reach it. There is nothing I can do but to cast myself upon forgiveness of God in Christ and leave it to him. This is where Calvary is precious.

Oh love divine, where shall my tongue its song of praise begin?

The precious blood of Christ my Lord has covered all my sin.

Now what shall I do with this bundle of habits that reaches down in that subliminal self about which I know so little? I know what it means to try to clear up that backyard and to find that the Ethiopian cannot at will change his color, or the leopard his spots. There is only one place to go. If I cast myself upon God, divine mercy with holy efficiency can change my life within, and then I begin to fight up-hill, for that is what repentance and forgiveness mean.

In Manchester, England, in the early days of the Salvation Army, at a time when the respectable public was very much against it, a Salvation Army lassie was taken into court, charged with impeding the traffic by holding a meeting on a public street. The judges were against her. The witnesses and the public were against her. On the bench, however, sat a judge, a thoughtful man of a distinct type. He heard the charge. He looked thoughtfully out of the window. "Obstructing the traffic?" "Yes." Looking at the girl, he said, "She has been guilty of obstructing the traffic on a very broad way where this court does not seem to have much jurisdiction," and taking off his gown, he laid it down, went down into the prisoner's dock and stood by her side and said, "I will stand with her through this trial." He meant, "As I look into the true inwardness of what this girl has done, I am on her side if all England is on the other side."

This is what Christ does for you and me. Knowing all the difficulties that confront us in overcoming our past and overcoming the tendency we have formed, knowing what an awful job we find on hand, the Judge himself comes and stands by our side in the dock and virtually says: "You have a hard row to hoe. You have made it hard for yourself, but I am going to stay by you, and we are going to fight it through together. Everything I have and all that I am is for you until the fight is done."

Now I am willing to tackle anything in the way of an uphill job in overcoming all that is in my own bosom if I can be sure that the great Saviour is by my side. That is repentance. There is nothing superficial about it. It does not mean simply, I have changed my mind and I am going in a different direction. It is not only the turning from sin but the work through life of replacing self-love with the love of Christ, and self-will with the will of Christ.

All these and much more he means when he says, "Thy sins are forgiven."

Sermon VIII

WHAT HE TAUGHT AND PRACTISED ABOUT PRAYER

Men ought always to pray.

> *Luke 18:1*

He prayed more earnestly.

> *Luke 22:44*

The teacher of religion today must make a choice between giving people what they *want* and what they really *need*. Alas, these two may be very far apart. The disposition to demand swift returns in satisfaction for all one's investments of time and effort leads us to shelve the deeper things of time and effort leads us to shelve the deeper things of life and live in the passing temporalities with the sad result of shallowness and flimsiness of character. In this, as in all else, Jesus stands out the incorruptible master teacher of all time. He knew that much that he said would not be fully appreciated for a long time, but the ages are his, and he can afford to wait. This morning I am asking you to take a new look at what he taught and practiced about prayer.

No one can read and listen attentively today without knowing that the thinking of even the Christian part of the world is in awful confusion at this point. First of all, a scientific understanding of the universe with its uniform laws has led many to jump to the conclusion that prayer is an impertinence or at best a useless effort. Very few would go as far as Mark Twain did in holding that;

> every event that ever took place here in the material universe or in the moral life of man was so wrapped up in the original atom with its potencies that nothing that has ever happened could possibly have turned out differently than it did down to the smallest detail.

But a great many thoughtful people have come to feel that if God is God of law and order, then we cannot expect him to alter the laws of a universe made in his own wisdom in order to change anything from its natural course, in answer to prayer. This frame of mind, of course, cuts the nerve of prayer at once.

There are other thoughtful persons who say, "Since God is all wise, what folly to keep interposing my little wishes, founded on the experience of a day, as amendments to the wisdom of him who has the everlasting ages behind him."

Before we try to answer these two propositions, for both of which a seemingly good argument can be set up, let us pause to admit frankly that if prayer is to be given up or simply reduced to "Thy will be done," then religion becomes a vastly different thing from what it is when we are sincere believers in and practisers of prayer. I will not say that religion without prayer is impossible, but I have no hesitation in saying that religious experience with prayer left out is a vastly different thing from religious experience with prayer given the place of honor at its very center.

Before we turn to the Master's view of prayer, let us add one other word. He never speaks as one who guesses or surmises or deals in probabilities. His teaching on prayer, like all the rest of his teaching, is positive and emphatic. It is the language of a lawgiver. He speaks as one who speaks for God and with God's full authority. Unless I can trust and follow him here, I cannot follow him at all.

He finds the reasonableness of prayer not by shutting his eyes to the facts, but rather in the revelation of life's inmost facts. He founds his doctrine on the very nature of things his bases are the nature and character of God, the nature and character of man, and the relation that exists between God and man. Jesus believed that God was sovereign, but not by any means an Oriental despot. He believed that man is subject and dependent, but not an automaton, rather a free spirit under a benign government. These things will appear more clearly as we proceed.

First of all, the Master declares that men ought always to pray. Let no one stumble over that word "always" as an impossible task. Prayer in his view is not a task at all but something infinitely deeper and closer to life. Men ought always to breathe. Do we make a task of that? Hardly. We breathe all day and never think of it at all until something goes wrong. What Jesus implies here is that just as breathing is part of the movement of our physical life, so prayer is part of the necessary and natural movement of the spiritual life. In breathing we do not go hunting for atmosphere. We simply accept the great, generous atmosphere that surrounds us as being ours, as being for us, and we proceed to breathe. So in the spiritual life. We are to accept God as him in whom we live and move and have our being, and make prayer the natural, glad, and constant expression of our relation to him. It is not the constant use of words the Master here means. The most prayerful man may use very few words. It is the constant attitude of the soul, not stained, but free and unconfined, of trust, love, expectation, and dependence. This is "praying always."

We have said that the Master founded his doctrine of prayer on the fundamental facts of existence, on the real nature of God, the real nature of man, and the relationship between God and man. Let us take one of his illustrations:

> Which of you that is a father, if his son shall ask bread, will he give him a stone? If he ask a fish, will he for a fish offer him a serpent, or if he ask an egg will he offer him a scorpion?

The implication here is that the relation between God and man is that of Father and child. The appeal is to human fatherhood, not human fatherhood at its best, but on the average. The conclusion is that when God answers prayer, he is only doing the natural thing, that as surely as an earthly father, even though far from perfect, will listen to the requests of his child, and grant them when possible, "How much more will your heavenly Father give good things to them that ask him?"

Immediately there arises the objection, Since God knows all, and our knowledge is so limited, what wisdom can there be in our asking and why should God be in any way affected by our asking? We have the Master's sanction for turning back again to human fatherhood. Watch the little boy and his father. It is true that the father knows a great deal more than the child, that he knows better than the child what is good for him, that many of the things the child asks the father would do irrespective of his asking, yet we expect to see the normal childhood and fatherhood, asking and giving. Even so, the argument that God knows so much and I know so little is not an argument against prayer at all. Our Lord Jesus frankly says, "Your Father knoweth what things ye have need of before ye ask," but he puts this forward not as a reason for refraining from prayer but as a reason for praying.

Turn to another: "Which of you shall have a friend." A friend is something different from a father. The feeling of fatherhood is founded upon relationship and responsibility. Friendship is entirely free and voluntary. Now note the Master's parable. You have a friend. You "knock at his door at midnight and say, Friend, lend me three loaves, for a friend of mine in his journey has come to me, and I have nothing to set before him." We are glad that the Master represents the pleader as asking not something for himself but for a hungry guest at his house "and he from within shall answer and say Trouble me not. The door is not shut and my children are with me in bed. I cannot rise and give thee."

Does he mean that God really talks this way to his child? No. But he does mean that very often to the praying soul the heavens appear like brass and it seems as if God were saying, "I cannot be bothered." Mark now the Master's conclusion, "I say unto you, [this is emphatic], though he will not rise and give him because he is his friend, yet because of his persistence he will arise and give him as many as he needeth."

Then does human persistence overcome God's reluctance? Not at all. There is no reluctance on the divine part, but he waits until our earnestness makes us sure of ourselves. He knows what we need. He waits until we are sure that we know that we really need it.

Take another: "There was a certain judge who neither feared God nor regarded man. There was in that city a poor widow." This is an amazing illustration—God represented under the figure of a judge who neither feared God nor regarded man. The suppliant is the most pitiable figure in that Oriental world, a poor widow. She comes with a prayer: "See that justice is done me by mine adversary." The judge pays no attention. She persists. At last he says "Though I fear not God nor regard man, yet because this woman pesters me, I will see that justice is done her rather than have her forever bothering me." What a strange illustration! What does it mean? Is God like that judge? No. He is exactly the opposite. The Master is using here an extreme illustration to the effect that if persistent pleading can overcome the indifference of a judge who has no love at all, what will persistent pleading do when dealing with such a one as our Father in heaven?

Another: "Two men went up into the temple to pray, the one a Pharisee, the other a publican." Note that these two men were taken, one from the extreme upper crust of the religious aristocracy of the Jewish world, and the other from the very bottom. The Pharisee was the standard, at least outwardly, of religious life. The tax-gatherer was a Jew who had lent himself to a heathen power to collect taxes from his fellow Jews to fill the coffers of Rome. He has sold himself to Satan. He was beyond the pale. These men both went up to the temple to pray. The Master's description of the Pharisee's prayer is the last word in divine sarcasm.

> He stood and prayed thus with himself: "God, I thank thee that I am not as other men are, extortioners, unjust, adulterers, or even as this tax-gatherer. I fast twice in the week. I give tithes of all that I possess."

In other words, he needed nothing. He came in to tell God what a good man he was. He exhibited all his patent virtues and went out with the comfortable sense of being a hundred percent before God as he was before men. The publican stood afar off, and did not lift up so much as his eyes to heaven but smote upon his breast, saying, "God have mercy on me for my sins." Here is a man with a sense of need. The Master says, "I tell you this man went down to his house accepted rather than the other."

What the Master is saying here is that one of the relations between God and man is that of a sinner and a Saviour. If we approach him as a child approaching a Father, as a friend a friend, as a sinner approaching a Saviour, and as needy soul approaching One whose resources are infinite and whose love is boundless, we shall find what Jesus found, that prayer is not only a theory but a fact, that we get a response. Let us follow in his footsteps.

Sermon IX

A SIMPLE DAY'S WORK

So he went preaching through the synagogues of Galilee

Luke 4:44

There fell into my hands this morning a book with a rather arresting title, *The Man Nobody Knows*. This title tells a great truth. If you could find the ripest saint on earth, the man or woman, most likely a woman, who knows the Master better than any other human soul, so far from thinking that he or she knows him entirely, you would find such an one conscious of a haunting sense of something unknown, far bigger than experience has yet covered, and coupled with this a great sense of gladness that he is too great to be known entirely. This does not mean that there is any doubt of what we do know. You can be more sure of Jesus Christ and of what you know of him than you can of any other person you have ever met. How important is this knowledge?

John Stuart Mill used to say, "Mankind cannot be too often reminded that a man named Socrates once lived."

I have no fault to find with this tribute to the ancient Greek sage, but a man might live a growing and successful life who never heard of Socrates, while no human life can come to its highest and best in ignorance of Jesus of

Nazareth. On the last night of his life, speaking to the Father in that prayer which constitutes a kind of a holy of holies in the Bible, he himself said, "This is life eternal, that they might know thee, the only true God, and Jesus Christ whom thou hast sent." If eternal life may be described as a blessed state of being begun on earth and continuing through eternity, and if the key to this experience is acquaintance with the Lord Jesus, then it is of no use to try to tell how important it is that we know him. It is more important to you and to me than any other privilege or responsibility we will ever face in this life. It is for this reason that we are devoting time to a study of the "Real Jesus" by attempting so far as possible to get through the encrustment of tradition that has covered his name during the centuries and see him as he really lived among men.

At the opening of the Galilean ministry, some five or six months after he first came before the public, the Gospel writers give in detail the story of a day's work. In the forenoon he healed a lunatic, in the afternoon a patient stricken with fever; in the evening he held a great free clinic in the street, healing all sorts of disease, physical and mental, and then after spending the night in prayer outside the town, he called on the disciples to come with him for a tour of similar service through the towns of Galilee.

First of all, may I ask you to notice that while his ministry was sprinkled with wonders of healing, his supreme calling was that of a preacher? He felt himself charged with a message from God. His preaching impressed everybody with its singular tone of authority. He appealed to no proofs among the sages of the past to buttress up what he said. Instead, he said, "Verily, verily, I say unto you." He considered that sufficient reason to give for anything. He preached in three ways, by what he said, by what he left unsaid, and by what he did, for his deeds of mercy were just another kind of preaching, preaching in action. With him action and message were so woven together that the deed and word reacted on each other, setting forth truth in a most startling and dramatic way.

Let us examine this day's work. In the forenoon he entered the synagogue. This was his favorite resort. Unlike the temple at Jerusalem, it had no animal sacrifices. It was a combination of village church and school, a place where people came together to hear the truth and to worship. In the congregation that morning appeared a lunatic. The sight of Jesus frenzied him. He began to shriek: "What have we to do with thee? I know thee, who thou art, the Holy One of God."

The people believed that this was a case of double personality, a man indwelt by a demon who so possessed him that he used this man's faculties of speech, etc., for his own wicked purposes. A modern expert psychologist would certainly diagnose the same case very differently. They did not know all about it then. We do not know all about it now.

But note the marvelous wisdom of the Master. He spoke his message not only in the speech, Aramaic, which they understood, but in the thought-forms to which they were accustomed. The one was as necessary as the other. Had he spoken in modern, scientific thought-forms, two thousand years would have passed before anybody would have understood what he was talking about. The greatness of Jesus was shown in that he accommodated his mighty message to the understanding of his hearers.

Let us bore down into the center of this story. Whatever else we may say, the man was degenerate. The Lord Jesus saw his need. What did he do? He brought the whole of God, might, wisdom, and love, to bear upon the whole of this man, body and spirit, in such a way that the man was restored to normality and became a partaker of the very peace of God. Every age will have its own theory of the "how" of it, but whatever they thought and whatever we think, one thing is clear, he saw the man's need, and actively bringing to bear upon him the resources of the divine nature. This is the miracle of Christ's power. I am glad I cannot explain him altogether. It would reduce him too near to my level. Here stands a man among men, so related to God that he can bring together the infinite resources of God's love and power and the need of the neediest in such a way as to produce this happy result.

Turn now to the second incident. From the synagogue he went to the house of Simon Peter. Here lay Peter's mother-in-law, parched with fever, probably delirious. What does he do? The same thing he did for the lunatic in the synagogue. He brought in his own person the fullness of God to bear upon her case, told her to arise, and in a few moments she was quietly ministering to them in full health and comfort. But the climax of the day is to come. Shades of evening gather. Can you see the little narrow street, filled with an excited throng? He is holding a free clinic in the open air. They come, the maimed, the blind, the deaf, the palsied, the leprous, the insane, some of their own accord, while others, more helpless, are brought by friends. He moves about among them. With keen, swift vision, he diagnoses every case and then with the lavish bounty of God, distributes to each according to his or her need until that hospital street is turned into a scene of universal rejoicing. His main business all day has been speaking the message of God. These deeds of mercy are simply the message in practice. The crowd is dispersed. Watch him yonder as he slips away to a lonely hillside and under the quiet stars, spends the night in prayer. I can hear him thanking God. I can hear him pleading for fresh reserves of power. I can hear him, with large and gracious sympathy, praying for the people, and above all, I can hear him say, "Father, thy kingdom come, thy will be done on earth as it is in heaven." With the return of the morning, the disciples come eagerly seeking him. "Master, Master, everybody is looking for you." His quiet answer was, "Come, we must go to the other village, for therefore am I sent," and throughout populous Galilee these scenes were repeated.

What does all this mean to us in the twentieth century? Jesus stands in our midst today, unseen. When I have found him, I have found the full religious value of God. I do not need to go any farther. He is the ultimate. There never can be a need in my life, nor in yours, nor in the complex which we call society that there is not a corresponding fullness in his power, wisdom, and grace to meet that need and bring the harmony of heaven on earth. When we receive him, trust him, surrender to him, tie up with him, God has a chance. Our lives become the channels of divine mercy, and his heart is satisfied.

Sermon X

THE VERY CORE OF CHRISTIANITY[1]

I am the vine, ye are the branches.

John 15:5

I have looked forward for weeks to this hour and occasionally I have been saying, "Now what kind of a message will be suitable for the day of dedication of the new building?" The first thought that came to me was that this building was built and is being dedicated for religious purposes; therefore I shall call your attention to some things that have to do with the very heart of our holy Christian religion.

I hope none of you will ever make the mistake of speaking or thinking in an apologetic way of the church as a religious institution. That is what the church is, and if we are not in that business, we have no reason for our existence. In some cities you would almost think that the church was a rival of the houses of entertainment, and that it was up to us to make our services as much like those of the house of entertainment as possible. God forbid! If that happens, I shall stop preaching and earn my living in some other honest way as you men and women in front of me are doing, for I certainly would be ashamed to have anything to do with such a church. Now, I am not casting any aspersions on houses that exist for the purpose of providing entertainment, but we are not in that business. The attraction of the house of God is a different attraction entirely.

One of the remarkable things about our Lord Jesus was the way he treated religion. Whether you take the lower view that he is the most remarkable man that ever lived, or the higher view that he is the divine Son of God, you must admit that he is the supreme exponent of religion on this earth from the dawn of creation until. In his treatment of religion there is something that I can only describe as absolutely charming. To Jesus, religion was not something apart from life; it was the core and center and very life of life; it touched everything; it bathed everything in its light. To him religion was the sweetest, the most natural, the most attractive, the most normal thing in all the universe. His way of treating religion was not to talk about it as an abstract thing, but to do everything he did, whether it was eating a meal, taking a walk, healing a sick person, or whatever it was, in the lights of the great truths of religion, and to him religion was real life.

What is the core of our Christianity? I think it will go without saying that there is a great deal of public talking and teaching that does not deal with the core of religion but with the fringe of trimmings. I beg you to come away from that, leave all disputed matters aside, leave out everything that is not essential to the heart of man, and ask what constitutes the heart, the very core of religion?

Someone says, "Isn't he going to take a text?" yes, I have a text, but first I want to attempt a definition of religion. What is religion? I don't know that anybody has ever been able to give a definition that will satisfy everyone, but let's attempt something broad enough to cover the ground in a general way, and yet not so broad as to be without meaning. Religion is the relationship of the soul to God and the kind of living that results from that relationship and grows out of it. I am not defining the Christian religion now, but religion in general, because I beg you to notice that folks have religion no matter where they may live or what kinds of gods they worship. It is as difficult to find a tribe without a religion as it is to find a tribe without language. It may be very crude, very low. Sometimes the low, the animistic, the crude, the almost brutal form the religion takes, is amazing. Nevertheless, that is the only religion the man had, and it is an expression of the relationship of the soul to God and the kind of living that results therefrom.

Then what is the Christian religion? Here we can be a great deal more definite. The Christian religion is the relationship of the soul to God interpreted through Christ, and the kind of living that results from that interpretation. Now mark the difference between a religious man and a Christian. A religious man believes that there is some kind of relationship between his soul and God, and his life bears the mark of that relationship. A Christian believes not simply that the human soul is related to God, but that the Lord Jesus Christ is the revelation of God, and that he is the Mediator through whom that relation is realized, and he tries to live the kind of a life that results from that kind of a relationship. I am casting no aspersions on any other religion when I say there is a vast difference between a person who simply believes he has a relationship with God and the man who believes that the Lord Jesus Christ is the very revelation of God.

I turn now to my text. Oh, I might have found many texts in the Bible that would have answered for this purpose, but this one seemed to me eminently satisfactory. It is found in the fifteenth chapter of John, at the fifth verse: "I am the vine, ye are the branches." It comes in the middle of the last tender, confidential talk the Master had with the disciples before he was crucified. I don't think they knew fully that the next day was to be the day of his death, but he knew it to a certainty, for the shadows were gathering. Mark the sweetness, charm, gentleness, intimacy of Jesus when he talked to them about their relationship to him and to the Father. Don't misunderstand what the shadows were. As far as Jesus was concerned, death had no shadow for him. He knew where he was going. A man who, when he was being crucified, would say, "Father, into thy hands I commend my spirit," who could go right through the garden, and through the valley of death and meet the Father face to face on the other side—our Lord Jesus Christ never would dread death as if it was a thing of shadows.

One day on the road he met a funeral procession. They were burying the only son of a widow. Jesus laid his hand on the bier, and said—and I think I can hear the tone in which he said it, a tone of authority combined with confidence in his heavenly Father—"Young man, I say unto thee, arise." And the dead man sat up and began to speak.

When brought into the death-chamber of a little child, he said, "She is not dead, but sleepeth," and they understood him so poorly that they laughed him to scorn. Then he asked that they be put out, and turning to the little, still form lying dead in the sense in which we use the word, he said, "Little girl, wake up." And she arose, and then, in such homely, friendly fashion, not forgetting material, practical things, he told them to give her some meat.

Once more. He is brought from away across the Jordan to Bethany, where Lazarus, the brother of Martha and Mary, lay dead. He had been in the grave four days. What now? He talks in the friendliest, most hopeful, sweetest way to the two sisters: "Thy brother shall rise again." They say, "I know that he shall rise again in the resurrection at the last day." They had the same idea about death that most folks still have, I am sorry to say. Jesus said, "I am the resurrection and the life." Martha, do you think the resurrection is a day? Nothing of the sort! The resurrection is a person. "I am the resurrection." Then he tells them to take away the stone, and again Martha hesitated. To break the seal of the place of death was a dreadful thing to a Jew. "Martha, didn't I tell you that if you would believe, you would see the glory of God?" They took away the stone, and Jesus, standing by the grave where the man had lain dead for four days, said, "Lazarus, come forth," and the dead man got up and walked out. Do you mean to tell me that death could put a shadow over Jesus when it was coming to him? Nothing of the sort. But he knew that he must bear the taunts and scorn of the very men he came to save, and that was enough to put a shadow on the face divine, and bathe the face of Christ with shame.

Now my text. It was spoken on the last night before he was crucified. The next day he will have passed away. What does he say? "I am the vine, ye are the branches." If there is a verse in the New Testament that goes straight to the heart of things in a practical way, it is this verse. He is using a figure of speech, so apt, so homely, so simple that a child can understand it, and yet a figure of speech that will bear looking at many times. Don't run away with the idea that you know what it means. You say, "A familiar verse; oh, yes, I know it." Know it? Are you sure? Men had seen apples fall from the trees for centuries before Sir Isaac Newton, but they did not understand the meaning of it until he saw an apple fall and began to quiz himself as to what it meant, and he thought through the law of gravitation. It is barely possible that if we will go back to an old text we know by heart so that we can say it backwards in our sleep, and take a new look at it reverently and thoughtfully, we may see something we never saw before.

Jesus is saying, "Come out into the vineyard."

Here is vine. I will take it and examine it. Three things are evident: First, branch and vine are united. The branch is fastened to the vine. Secondly, it is evident to everyone who has watched vines grow that there is something that passes over from the vine to the branches. You say it is sap. Someone who looks deeper says it is life. Yes, it is sap that bears the life. Thirdly, the vine bears fruit because it is fastened to the branch and receives that life. If I mistake not, it is these three things that the Master had in mind when he said, "I am the vine, ye are the branches."

Let us apply them and see what the Master meant. First, that the believing soul is united to Christ, that there is a real union between the soul and Christ. How folks have misunderstood religion! I have met people, and pretty intelligent-looking people too, who thought that being a Christian consisted in about four or five "don'ts." I could mention some of them, but I forbear. "If you don't do this, and don't do that other, then I guess you are a Christian." You couldn't make a Christian out of a million "don'ts." There are not "don'ts" enough in the universe to make one Christian. It isn't because you don't do this or that that you are a Christian. I know there are some things in this world that no one should do, certainly no Christian, but there is only one thing that can make you a Christian, and that is if you are really united to him who came down from heaven to be your Saviour, who lived for you, who died for you, and now is at the right hand of God interceding for you.

Union with Christ is the central article of faith in Christ. In these days we ask, what is fundamental? What is bedrock? What is the thing by which the soul of man lives? Never mind the trimmings. I won't be lost if I don't have the trimmings, and I won't be saved if I have them. What is fundamental? I have come to it now. Unless your soul is united to the living Christ, you are not saved. No creed, no ritual, no ordinance, nothing except to be united to Christ. By what sort of a union? It is a union by faith.

Someone says, "We have got into the realm of fog, all right." Not at all. Faith is taking Christ as if he were real, and treating him as if he were real. Someone says, "Prove it to me." You cannot prove the things of Christ as you prove a mathematical proposition. I am shy of many of the things that are brought forth as proofs of Christianity. Faith is a venture, and you cannot make anything else of it, and you cannot make anything less of it. If you will allow me a modern word, in order to prove Christ in real Christian fashion, a man must be a "good sport." He has to have a little of the dare in him. It is stepping out on the unseen. I have never seen Jesus with these eyes; I have never touched him with these hands.

> Jesus, these eyes have never seen
> That radiant form of thine;
> The veil of sense hangs dark between
> Thy blessed face and mine,
>
> I see thee not; I hear thee not,
> Yet thou art oft with me,
> And earth has ne'er so dear a spot
> As where I meet with thee.

What is the writer describing in that hymn? He is describing the experience of the soul's union with Christ, the

65

experience of the man or woman who says: "I know I cannot see him. I cannot prove that he is real, but I believe he is real, and I am going to take him and obey him and trust him and follow him as if he were real, and I believe I shall prove before I get through that he is real." That is faith. It is greeting the unseen with a cheer; it is treating the unseen Saviour as if he were real, and that is the way in which we prove that he is real.

> The steps of faith fall on the seeming void
> And find the rock beneath.

In our boyhood days, sometimes it was necessary to ride a horse through a stream. We had a suspicion how deep that stream was, but we did not always know, and the horse did not always know, and sometimes it was a toss-up which was more frightened, the horse or the boy on his back. I can feel him now, picking his way carefully through the stream. He couldn't see his way, but he believed there was bottom there, and I believed there was bottom there, and I pushed him on, and sure enough, before long we were coming up on the other side.

Christ's way of uniting the soul to him puts all men on a level. It matters not how much a man knows, it matters not how ignorant a man is, there is only one way he can do business with the Lord, Jesus, and that is to try. The person may be one who cannot read or write, like the Lahus faraway up yonder in eastern Burma, with no written language, knowing nothing of the background of your life and mine. When that man is told of Jesus, all he needs to do is to say, "I believe he is real." Have any of you ever found any other way by which a person can be united to Christ?

You cannot be united to him by doing a heap of good work here. You cannot be united to him by what other people have said about time. You cannot take your faith as a hand-me-down from a mother or father or Sunday-school teacher. No, every man has to make the venture for himself.

Now the second thing. This simple figure teaches us that when the soul unites itself to Christ by faith and says, "Lord, I believe you are real; your way of life is the best and I am going to trust you"—when the soul does that, the something follows, namely, something passes over from Christ to the believing soul, not once for all like a Christmas gift, take it or leave it as you choose, not once for all, but a steady stream of giving, of imparting himself to the believing soul. Thus does Christ hand over his life to us.

> Moment by moment I'm kept in his love,
> Moment by moment I've life from above.

It is continual, permanent experience, the experience of living with Christ and letting Christ live with you. Someone says, "Are you not in the realm of mystery?" Yes, but not any more than you are in the realm of mystery when you speak of other things. Will you tell me how you do your thinking? What is the thing you have in the top of your head that you think with? How do you think? What is that someone says, "Mystery?" Yes. If I know perfectly well that there is a process of thinking going on in myself that I cannot describe or analyze or fathom or get to the bottom of in a thousand years, then why should I stumble to know that as I look into the face of an unseen Saviour, he somehow or other imparts himself and his life to the believing soul? I am describing Christian experience, not the outside trimmings, but the thing itself, the thing that really enables you to be a Christian.

Go back to the vineyard and look again. That branch, without making any noise, without advertising it, is busy all the time receiving; that vine is busy all the time giving out life.

Now, the third point. We felt yonder in the vineyard that the vine that receives life from the branch has results, and the results can be seen by everyone. That vine bears fruit. What is this the Master says? "He that abideth in me, and I in him, the same bringeth forth much fruit." Master, what kind of fruit do you expect if I live in fellowship with you? The answer is so plain that he who runs may read. Let us analyze it. Two things are evident about the righteous life: (1) It is a life of purity; (2) it is a life of love. If we want to test ourselves by God's plummet, here is the way. How far am I living a life of purity, and how far am I living a life of love—not simply a life of friendliness with those who just suit me? Anybody can be friendly with people who just suit them, but how far am I living the life of love toward people who do not just suit me? Here are two tests of the kind of fruit the Master calls for.

Now, dear friends, I tell you the thing that persuades me to remain in the ministry is my profound belief that if we unite ourselves to Christ by faith and thus allow him to put across to us his own indwelling life, this kind of fruit becomes possible to all of us until the soul will overflow with blessing to all around.

I remember hearing Doctor Mabie tell of seeing a baptism in the Telugu country in India. The service was all in Telugu, of which he could not speak a word. A woman of mature years was being baptized, a woman, worn, shoulders bowed, hands knotted with toil, not a very intelligent-looking face, just one of the common herd, one of the backward underlings of the heathen world. The missionary asked a question which Doctor Mabie could not understand, and when she replied, though he could not tell a word she was saying, Doctor Mabie said: "I would have taken my oath on what I saw on her face that the image of Jesus was in her heart and that she was in love with Jesus Christ. There was a look on her face that could never be imitated or counterfeited." It was "the light that never was on sea or land." He knew by what he saw that she had received life from Christ. All over this world this miracle is taking place, and to this, and to everything that grows therefrom this building is dedicated.

I believe I would be wrong if I did not give an opportunity to the hesitant to make this decision, if I did not ask you to make this an hour of real decision in your own heart. Hark, now. Are you persuaded that Christ is the Son of God and that he came to be your Saviour? Someone says, "I rather think that is so." Are you persuaded that the next step is yours, and that by uniting yourself to him, the blessing he came to bring can be yours? Do you know that the only way to treat Jesus Christ is to treat him as real? Will you make this day the beginning? Master, I will walk out of this building today with a high determination that I will treat you as real. If you do, then three things will be true: Your soul will be united to Christ; he will impart himself to you, giving you of his spirit, clothing your life with the beauty that comes from him; and that other glorious thing, that while you cannot bring forth fruit of yourself, he will enable you to bring forth much fruit.

The Real Jesus

We will pause a moment in thy presence, Master, that the determination may be recorded in our hearts, that we may have a chance to stick down our stake and say, "Lord Jesus, we will take thee to be real and treat thee as real, and we will ask what is the first step of obedience and we will do it, and what is the next step and we will do it, and thou wilt lead us on." And, oh, Master, we pray that no one of us may be satisfied unless our lives are bringing forth the kind of fruit that will satisfy thee. We ask it through Jesus Christ, our Lord.

Sermon XI

IS IT AT ALL POSSIBLE TO BE LIKE JESUS CHRIST?

For whom he did foreknow, he also did predestinate to be conformed to the image of his Son.

Romans 8:29

"For whom he did foreknow, he also did predestinate to be conformed to the image of his Son." A moment's thought, and you will see that this is a very startling phrase indeed. It leads me to ask, is it at all possible for folks like you and me to be like Christ in any great degree? The first suggestion that came to me when I read the text was this: Either this man had a very low conception of Christ, or else he had a very high conception of humanity and its possibilities. He is either bringing the Lord Jesus Christ down to a very low level, or else he is calling upon us to take a great flight, to get up on the level where Jesus lived. It doesn't disturb some people to contemplate this. There are some who do not have any trouble because they regard Jesus as just a bit better than other men; all you have to do is just give yourself to it, and you can rise to his level.

But I beg you to notice that the man who wrote this verse was not bringing the Lord Jesus Christ down to accommodate human weakness and sin. He had an infinitely high idea of the greatness of Christ. Probably no disciple ever had such a lofty conception of Christ as the man who wrote these words. Hear how he talks: "In him dwelleth all the fullness of the Godhead bodily," as if to say, "When you see Christ, you see the moral character of God without a flaw." No, he does not belittle Christ. Then I am forced to the other conclusion, that the writer of this verse was a man who believed that humanity was capable of tremendous improvement. He did not believe that Jesus needed to be brought down, but that you and I are capable of rising to heights that can hardly be expressed.

In what kind of human society did this disciple, Paul, live? He must have lived among very fine folks if he thought they were capable of becoming like Christ. He lived in the first century of the Christian era, in that old Roman world. We sometimes think that things are pretty bad now, and sometimes you will hear a man declare that society today is going down-hill. All we would need to do for that man would be to lift him right up, take him back 2,000 years, and set him down in the midst of society in which Paul lived. Leave him for one week in the midst of that old Roman society, and at the end of the week he would say: "Take me back. I didn't know the world was so good." The decencies of speech would forbid one even from trying to put before you the kind of society in which Paul lived.

On that hard Roman world
Disgust and secret loathing fell,
Deep weariness and sated lust
Made human life a hell.

And yet right out of the muck and rottenness of this Roman world, the apostle wrote that it was possible for a man to become more and more like Jesus Christ until he was conformed to the image of the one "in whom dwelleth all the fullness of the Godhead bodily." "Paul, where do you get your faith in humanity, such boundless faith as this?" I turn back to the verse again and make a discovery. He gets his faith in the improvableness—mark the word—the *improvableness* of humanity from God's own faith therein. He believed it because God believes it.

Read the verse once more. "For whom he did foreknow, he also did predestinate to be conformed to the image of his Son." Paul is saying, "I am going back to the ground-plan of the universe, to what was in God's mind when he made humanity." Men may be mistaken, but God cannot be. How much does God believe in humanity? He believes so much in humanity and in its improvableness that he sent into the world his own Son with the expectation that men and women would catch from Christ the divine fire and grow to be like him. It is pretty safe to believe anything God believes, and we go back to bedrock, to the very ground-plan of the universe when we believe what God does. Paul says: "My back is to the wall. I stand for God's plan: I find that God built the world this way, that men should be conformed to Christ's image, and I believe even the worst men can become like Christ because God declares it."

A poor illiterate woman, who kept a house of ill-repute in one of our Southern California towns, was dragged into court on a Monday morning because of her misdeeds, again the next Monday morning, and the next, until her poor, sodden face was a familiar sight in that court. One day somebody preached Christ to her. What now? She is the financial secretary of the Baptist church and the most trusted woman in the community, trusted alike by white folks and black. Our Baptist Society sends its money by hundreds of dollars to that woman for the carrying on of its work. What did it? An ignorant, vicious woman, who had lived on the animal plane, and sunk lower than I care to tell—if that could happen to her, then I do not wonder that Paul could fall back on God's promise and believe that from all eternity he built this wonder into the ground-plan of the world.

What he is saying is that this is no doubtful experiment, that the gospel is the power of God to lift men, from the depths of their sin and degradation, toward and *toward* and TOWARD the very likeness of Jesus Christ. You will not realize how much this means unless you walk up alongside of Jesus Christ and do a little comparing.

I see this man, in the stainless purity of his life, going through communities where everything was muck. I look at him in the midst of men, suspicious, grasping, greedy, and who will to do other men to the death in order to advance their own interests, and lo, he looks out for everybody else, himself taking the lowest place. I look at him in the midst of the storms that beat upon him and I find him as calm and steady as if nothing had happened. When the time came for him to walk down the Valley of the Shadow of Death, he walked straight toward his cross as if he were going to a crown, and said, "Father, forgive them; for they know not what they do," "Father, into thy hands I commend my spirit." Walk up alongside of him and look. I will do the same, and if it doesn't take the conceit out of us, nothing in heaven above or earth below ever will.

Someone says: "That only discourages me. You started to preach on 'Is it possible to become like Christ?' " It is not possible for anybody to become like Christ by attending to the trimmings and edges and outside appearance of life. A Christian is not a copyist, and there is only one way we can become like Christ, and that is to have something happen in *here*, in the depth of your spirit. While we have bodies that are very useful, and we are joined to them for the present, and the way we use them makes or unmakes us, we are something more than bodies. You are a spirit, made in the image of God, and it is because you, the real you, are in spirit, made in the image of God, that it is possible for God to say some tremendous things to you as in this text.

There is only one way whereby I can become like Christ. It is not by slavishly copying how he did this, that, or the other, but by having my spirit gripped by his spirit and bathed in his spirit. The Bible says when two people are married, "they are no more twain, but one flesh"; this is what makes divorce such a horrible thing even when it is necessary. "But he that is joined unto the Lord is one spirit." That is to say, real conversion is a marriage of your spirit and God's spirit in such a way that you are no more two but one. The only way in which a human being can become like Christ, is by having the inner spirit, the heart of your heart, the life of your life gripped and embraced by his spirit and united to him by faith and love. How in the world can that be? How can I get into that kind of embrace with God? What can we do to establish the relationship?

Do you remember the story in the New Testament of a certain centurion who came to Jesus and said: "My servant lies at home sick of the palsy, grievously tormented. Come and do something for him." Jesus said, "I will come," and the man began to shake with fear, and said: "I am not worthy; you don't need to come under my roof. Just speak the word, and my servant will be healed. I know how it is, for I am a man under authority, having soldiers under me, and I say to this man, 'Go,' and he goeth, and to another, 'Come,' and he cometh, and to my servant, 'Do this,' and he doeth it." Jesus turned to the people around and said, "I have not found faith like that before in all Israel."

Let's examine that man's faith. He was not looking at what he could do. He was looking at what Jesus could do, and he had such an extravagant notion of what Jesus could do that he said, "You need not come under my roof." In other words, he believed his servant could be healed by a word because he had such profound faith that Jesus could do anything.

You or I approach the Lord Jesus. What shall I ask? "Master, I can't make any change in my inner spirit by my own power. I can't change the complexion of my heart; I can't purify I can't sanctify my life by my own power any more than I can pull myself up-stairs by my bootstraps; but instead of looking at what I can do, I will look at thee. In thee is the power of God—enough! In thee is the wisdom of God—enough, and everything there is in God meets in thee and thou hast come to be the Saviour of a sinner like me. There is one thing I can do. I can surrender my spirit to thee, and I can believe that thou wilt grip, embrace, enfold, and take possession of me, and that which I cannot do or hope to do for myself, thou wilt do."

A lady had some seeds in a pot. They were not doing very well, and she said, "I will put them on the side of the house where the sun shines." In a few days they were growing beautifully. What had she done? Forced the growth of seeds? No; you cannot force life. She put them where the sun, ninety-five millions of miles away, could shine upon them and stir them to life. What can I do with my life? I can put it where the Sun of Righteousness can get at it by surrendering to him and believing what he believes concerning me.

There is one kind of optimism that is just the overflowing of high hopes in youth. It does not get what it hopes for. There is another kind that reasons this way: Let me find out first how much Christ believes in me, what he thinks of me and my capabilities. It is perfectly safe to believe anything he believes concerning me. I say, "Master, what do you believe of me?" and he says, "I believe you are capable of becoming like me." "Master, do you mean it?" "I believe you are capable of becoming like me." "Then, Lord Jesus, if you believe that, I will dare to believe it, and I will give the Sun of Righteousness a chance at the seed-plot of my life, I will bare my spirit to him and wait on him."

A man needs only one conversion but many renewals. What is conversion? It is turning around and facing in an opposite direction. You have not changed your inner spirit by turning from west to east. Regeneration is more than turning around. It is being born again. We need only one conversion but many rebirths. Oh, I know there is one conversion when the soul is first introduced to Christ. There is never any other like that. But, there is a process by which the soul is continually filled with Christ's spirit, is continually being born again. Let me quote from our hymn-book. Not all hymns are good theology, but this one is:

> Oh, Jesus Christ, grow thou in me,
>   And all things else recede;
> My heart be daily nearer thee,
>   From sin be daily freed.

I know no other secret of getting it except to begin the day with it and close the day with it, and every time the sense of need comes, to go back to it, to surrender my inner spirit to Christ, and as he works in me, to believe that he will clothe my life with the beauty and virtue of his own, that he will help me to will as he wills, think as he thinks, feel as he feels, see as he sees, love as he loves, move as he moves, and so reproduce something of his own glorious, divine life in me.

Hark! If all mankind today were to begin to believe in themselves and in the possibilities of improvement in them as God believes in us; if you, for the next week, would believe in your own possibilities of improvement as God believes in you right now, what would happen? That would mean to commit yourself to God entirely and for him to do not what you would imagine possible, but what he believes possible.

Look at Simon Peter by the Sea of Galilee. He was a pretty rough kind of man. After he had been with the Master three years, he slipped a cog and ripped out an oath and lied like a trooper. What kind of man had he been before he joined the Master that he could do that now? No nice little polished Sunday-school product. He had been pretty rough. I will take Simon Peter a few days before Jesus met him and say: "I had a dream about you last night, Simon Peter. I dreamed that a day was coming when your life would be so changed, when you would be so enraptured with the Spirit of God, when you would be so one with God that you would stand up before a hostile mob and tell them about Jesus, and you would win them over, three thousand at a time. I dreamed that." He would say: "What kind of dope did you take before you went to bed? That's utterly impossible. I am not capable of doing anything of the kind." The day came when he did that very thing. How? By the indwelling of Christ.

Is it possible for us to be at all like Christ? If it isn't, this building of churches is just wasting our time. The whole thing falls to the ground unless this is true. If it is true, how would it do for each of us, individually, to pull ourselves together and say: "Master, I know in a measure what I am, and I am not very proud of it. All I have to do to bring me to a sense of what I am is to walk up alongside of you and have my picture taken with yours. But I am going to look at myself from your point of view because you came from heaven to be my Saviour, because you invested your own life-blood in my redemption. Do you really believe that I am capable of becoming like you?" If I ask that, only one answer can come back. The Lord Jesus Christ will say: "Yes, I saw from eternity what you are capable of becoming. I knew it before I came from heaven. I have known it every step of your crooked and wayward life, and I have come to bring to you the means by which you can rise until you become like me. I in you, and you in me; I dwelling in your spirit, and you trusting me, believing me, listening to my voice, looking up to me as a servant to his master, as a maiden to her mistress, as a pupil to the teacher, making room for me, and above all by believing that I can do in you that which I have undertaken."

If I should take a vote, print ballots reading thus, "Do you believe that the Lord Jesus can do in your own person, really, that thing he says he can do? Please write 'Yes' or 'No'"—what would you write? If you wrote "Yes," do you see what you are committed to? If you wrote "No," do you see where it places you? If we write "Yes," there is only one logical thing for us to do, and that is to say: "Master, if this is possible, and if it is the supreme thing in the universe, then lead me to it. Let me surrender myself now to thee, today, tomorrow, each day, until the habit of surrender shall have become a dominant habit of my life, and let me believe this great fact until it shall be the beginning and middle and end of my creed, that Jesus Christ is able to grip me and take possession of me and do for me that which I cannot do for myself."

Out of my bondage, sorrow and night,
    Jesus, I come; Jesus, I come;
Into thy freedom, gladness, and light,
    Jesus, I come to thee;
Out of my sickness into thy health,
Out of my want and into thy wealth,
Out of my sin and into thyself,
    Jesus, I come to thee.

Oh, hear us, Master, as we come before thee this morning with all our weakness and sins, with the sins that our neighbors know and the darker ones that no one else knows but thee, with the plagues of our lives that no one sees but God. We come and ask that thou wilt give us a strong, steady faith that thou wilt work in us until we become like thee, that in place of our selfishness thou wilt put thine unselfishness, that instead of our suspiciousness there may be wrought out in us something of the kind of faith in men that thou dost have. Grant that when it comes to things physical hindering us from being brought under the Spirit, as thou didst use the body as a servant, so may we never allow it to dominate. We pray for anyone who is tempted to be discouraged and say, "Well, others may become like Jesus, but it is too late for me." Lord Jesus, whisper to such that they have never fairly tried thee, and that thou, the living Son of God, never didst turn anybody away. We pray that we may go from this building yielding ourselves to thee in such a way that the radiance of Christ shall find expression through us all our days. Amen.

Sermon XII

(Coronation Sermon at the B.Y.P.U. Convention,
Los Angeles, Ca., Sunday evening, July 11, 1926)

ARISE, SIR KNIGHT!

*All authority hath been given unto me in heaven
and in earth. Go ye therefore, and teach all
nations, baptizing them in the name of the
Father, and of the Son, and of the Holy Spirit;
teaching them to observe all things whatsoever I
commanded you; and, lo, I am with you always,
even unto the end of the world.*

Matthew 28:18-20

This is a very joyful and significant occasion. I am
thinking of that old scripture, "And they shall come from
the east and from the west, and from the north and from the
south." They are here. "And shall sit down with Abraham,
Isaac, and Jacob." These three gentlemen will not appear
tonight, the reason being, as someone has said, that they have
taken their letters to another church. I congratulate you on the
character of this convention. Instead of coming to its simply
to listen to a few platform speeches, and then say, "Now it is
all done, we will go home," you came together principally to
gather in these group conferences of which we have been
hearing and to focus your attention upon Christ's work in the
world. That is worth infinitely more to you than to listen to a
lot of addresses. You have had a great convention—lots of

fun, lots of good fellowship, splendid teaching, and great inspirational addresses. You are going away with fond memories of California and of each other, and this is going to be a milestone to which you will look back for a long time. I take it for granted that, in these closing moments you would want me to talk as a serious man to serious men and women.

If you will go out on a clear night and look up, you will see flung across the sky something that looks like a great river of stars. We call it the "Milky Way." They are not planets like this little ball on which we live. They are mighty suns shining by their own light. Many of them are a million times as big as this world, and there are more than a thousand million of them. They look from this distance as if they were close together. As a matter of fact they are so far apart that if two of them had been approaching each other at the beginning of human history at the rate of four hundred million miles a year, they would not have advanced far enough by the present time so that their position in relation to each other would seem materially altered. The human mind breaks down when it tries to think of the vastness of it all but there is one thing far more wonderful than the universe, and that is the one who is behind it, the everlasting God.

An inspired writer once said, "When I behold the heavens, the work of thy fingers, the moon and the stars, which thou hast ordained; what is man, that thou art mindful of him, or the son of man that thou visitest him?" The answer to this great query is furnished in history, furnished by the greatest fact we know, the greatest thing that any mortal ever believed. It makes the reverent heart stand still with awe. It is this: the everlasting God who has created and who upholds the universe, chose to become one of our human race. To believe this is the most daring adventure of faith ever taken and is beyond question the greatest thing ever believed by man.

Let us turn now to the story. A child is born in an obscure village. He is brought up in another obscure village. He works in a carpenter shop until he is thirty, and then for three brief years is an itinerant preacher, proclaiming a message and living a life. He never writes a book. He never holds an office. He never raises an army. He never has a family of his own. He never owns a home. He never goes to college. He never travels two hundred miles from the place where he was born. He gathers a little group of friends about him and teaches them his way of life. While still a young man the tide of popular feeling turns against him. The band of followers forsakes him. One denies him; another betrays him. He is turned over to his enemies. He goes through the mockery of a trial; he is nailed on a cross between two thieves, and when dead is laid in a borrowed grave by the kindness of a friend.

Those are the facts of his human life. He rises from the dead. Today we look back across nineteen hundred years and ask, what kind of a trail has he left across the centuries? When we try to sum up his influence, all the armies that ever marched, all the parliaments that ever sat, all the kings that ever reigned are absolutely picayune in their influence on mankind compared with that of this one solitary life. He has changed the moral climate of the world, and he is changing it now, and will continue to do so until the kingdoms of this world shall become the kingdom of our Lord and of his Christ. I ask you to pause a moment and think of this thing which Christians believe. We are talking about great adventures. I remind you that there must be a great adventure in faith before there can be a great adventure in faith before there can be a great adventure in action. No man has ever done a great thing until he has first believed a great thing.

I come now to the great call that he has issued to his followers in this world. After he had lived his life, after he had wrought his miracles, after he had calmly and gloriously passed through the grave and stood on heaven's side of an empty tomb, he called his disciples together and gave them their marching orders. If any greater words have ever been uttered on this earth, we have not heard them. He said:

> All authority hath been given unto me in heaven and on earth. Go ye, therefore, and make disciples of all nations, baptizing them in the name of the Father, the Son, and the Holy Spirit, teaching them to observe all things whatsoever I have commanded you, and lo, I am with you always, even unto the end of the world.

I will ask you to notice three things in this tremendous statement, which we call the Great Commission. The first is the place and authority which he assumes for himself. The second is the command which he gives his followers. The third is the infinitely precious and age-long promise that accompanies the command.

Look first at *the place and authority that he claims for himself.* We have a word in our modern speech that is all right in its place. We talk about "boosting" men. Jesus Christ was not a booster, and he does not ask that men boost him. The night before he died, in an upper room, he did something that left its impression upon the world for all time. He girded himself with a towel and deliberately washed the feet of his disciples, and when one of them objected, he said: "You call me Master and Lord; and you say well; for so I am. If I then, your Lord and Master, have washed your feet, you also ought to wash one another's feet." That man, who girded himself with a towel in the fashion of a servant, stooped down and washed the feet of his disciples, is the same man who stands up and says calmly and deliberately, as if he were uttering a commonplace thing that everyone ought to know, "All authority hath been given unto me in heaven and on earth."

We need not try to make any comparison between the authority of Jesus Christ and that of any one else. He is an authority without any peer. It is an authority that is not bounded by time or place. It is the authority of eternity. It is the authority of God. It is the authority of infinite righteousness. It is the one authority above all others, and what we need is not to boost Jesus Christ but to discover him, not to boost him but to give him the place that rightly belongs to him, and take our stand under his authority. But I beg you to notice what that means for you. A moment ago I asked you to look at the vastness of the universe. When you adventure into Christian service under the Lord Jesus, you not only have the backing of the universe, but you have the backing of the One who is back of the universe. We are working according to the ground-plan of God. He who framed the world invites us to work by this plan. He will yet succeed in accomplishing all that he has planned.

I will ask you now to look at *the command*: "Go ye, therefore, and make disciples of all the nations, teaching them to observe all things whatsoever I have commanded you." I beg you to notice this is worldwide in its scope and age-long in its duration. It naturally divides itself into two phases. In discipling the nations, there is first the winning of individual souls to Christ, and I am going to ask this great body of young people, you who have taken the name of Jesus, who call yourselves his followers, are any of you going to be satisfied to live your life and leave the world without winning some one individual yourself to allegiance to Christ? Are you willing to think of leaving this world and its opportunity for Christian service with an absolutely starless crown? I have no manner of doubt that every young man and woman here, if you set your mind and heart to it, can have the privilege of knowing that someone has been won to Christ by you.

Will you pardon a personality? This morning at the close of the service, a stranger from a distant state came up, introduced himself, and said: "I had a boy who lived down here in Southern California a few years ago and attended your church. The impress you made upon him has changed the whole course of his life, and I thought you would be glad to know it." Was I glad? I have been thanking God all the rest of the day for that sweet thing that was said to me this morning. That experience can be your own.

But there is another side to this great command besides winning individuals. India, after a century and a quarter of missionary work, has over four millions of Christians, and 325 millions who are not yet Christians, but the thinking, feeling, and ideals of the 325 millions have been radically altered by the presence of Christ in India and by the preaching of his gospel during this century and a quarter. Things so bad that the decencies of speech forbid mentioning them, that were commonplaces in social life in that land one hundred years ago, will never be tolerated in India again. They have been banished by the Spirit of Christ. So the kingdom of God grows not alone by the winning of one and one and one, but by permeation and diffusion. It is like the coming of spring. It is like the influence that a mighty magnet exerts on all around it. It is the very breath of God in human life, bringing the kingdom in its completeness nearer and nearer. Christ permeates and interpenetrates the thinking of the masses of this world until it is changed into the very kingdom of God.

Two children are born on the same day in two separate homes. So far as anyone can see they are equal in heritage, in ability, in prospect. One of them is born into a home where love reigns, where father and mother respect and love each other, where God is reverenced, where service for others, both in the home and outside, is life's main business. The other is born into a home where instead of love there is a snarl, there is selfishness, there is impurity, there is strife, there is everything that ought not to be. One of these children is damned in his cradle by his surroundings. The other has a thousand chances to one for a splendid, developing, righteous life. Why? The difference is in the atmosphere into which they were born. It is just as much your business and mine to complete what Jesus began, in changing the moral climate of the world, as it is to win individuals to Christ. Now I beg you to remember that the only way you can do either one of those things is by having the great Christ enshrined and reincarnated in your own life. Christ rides into this world, not alone through a printed page, not through statutes, or organizations, but supremely through personality. If God could not get as close to human life as he wanted except by taking the form of man, then you cannot reach people except through your personality. You cannot expect that your influence is going to be any better than you are. You must be an incarnation of the thing you say, or the thing you are will thunder so loud folks cannot hear what you say. Don't let the thing you are contradict the thing you say. As we deal with people, they watch the things we do much more closely than the things we say. This is our tremendous adventure, to obey the command of Christ. We do not have to invent anything. We take that which the Master has laid before us and say,

"Lord Jesus, I will go forward with thee, and by thy grace I will consecrate all I am and all I can be to carrying out this program which thou hast begun."

I beg you to notice that the Master also said, "Baptize them." I am here tonight as a Baptist and make no apology for it. You and I are speaking as Baptists. The more I observe the great ordinance of baptism, the more I am filled with delight at the wisdom of Jesus Christ in appointing that ordinance of baptism, so simple and so splendid. Words have to be translated from language to language, and sometimes the translation is very awkward, but an act translates itself. When you yield yourself to be buried beneath the water and rise again according to the command of the Lord Jesus Christ, you are saying a very glorious and significant thing. You are saying: "Master, I believe that thou didst die for me and that thou didst rise again, and here and now I yield myself to thee. I believe that I am so bound up in the bundle of life with the Lord that I reckon myself dead to the old life and arise to a new world, and in this new world thou, Christ, art all in all."

Then he goes on to say, "Teach them to observe all things whatsoever I have commanded you." There are some things about the life of Christ, about his coming into this world, that are beyond our understanding. We are dealing with the mighty mystery of the eternal. I wonder if any of you are troubled by all the talk about the supernatural or natural birth of Christ. An individual says to me, "I believe Christ had two human parents." My answer is this: It would take just as much of God and just as much of a miracle to produce a Jesus Christ through two human parents as through one, and I know so little of the processes of the eternal that I am not disposed to spend my time quibbling. I will leave that to him, and yield myself to his mastership and leadership for

88

all time. Do not spend any time disputing about the things concerning which nobody knows anything except what are we told in the word of God.

Now let us come to the *promise* that goes with this tremendous command. "Lo, I am with you always, even unto the end of the world." The Master here assumes that he is alive from the dead and is speaking to us from beyond the grave. Here again we are confronted by mystery. Someone raises all kinds of questions about the resurrection. I do not know anything about the nature of the resurrection. I know that they nailed him to a cross. I know that they took him down a dead man and laid him in Joseph's tomb. I know that on the morning of the third day they found the grave empty except for the grave-clothes, and I know that he made himself known to them—I mean to their human sense—as being alive, now to one, now to two, now to seven, then to one hundred and twenty, and finally to five hundred; at least eleven separate manifestations of himself were given during forty days. What does this mean? It means that the living Christ is as near to you young people here tonight as he was to the generations that walked on earth when he was here. "I am with you all the days." Someone has said that there are thirty-two thousand promises in the Bible. I never counted them, but here is one promise that is as if the Master took all the promises of power, of strength and rolled them into one great bundle, saying, "I am with you."

You are going out into this great adventure. It is the thing that will dignify life. It is the thing that will enable you to leave to leave your mark on the ages. As you go, there comes from the unseen a voice of infinite authority and infinite tenderness, and it says to you and to me everything that we need, "Lo, I am with you." As you go to your home, it is your privilege to have him as your companion and under all the stress and trial of life, it is your privilege to hear him say, "Lo, I am with you." This is the real knighthood. Let us highly resolve: "Lord Jesus, I will not disappoint thee. I have taken thy name, and now I give thee my heart and my hand for all time."

www.ingramcontent.com/pod-product-compliance
Lightning Source LLC
LaVergne TN
LVHW011214080426
835508LV00007B/783